YOUR DEFINING MOMENT

YOUR DEFINING

MOMENT

WHEN TIME AND DESTINY MEET

JEN TRINGALE

Harrison House
Tulsa, OK

Your Defining Moment
Copyright © 2015 Jen Tringale
ISBN: 978-168031-032-0
Published by Harrison House Publishers
Literary Agent: Bush Publishing & Associates
Cover Art by Artworks Photography of Tulsa

CONTENTS

ENDORSEMENTS

I have always believed and taught that God has something for every believer to do, something more than just sitting in the church pew or standing behind a pulpit. The Church isn't a building where people meet for preaching, teaching, and worship. The Church is people who love and serve Jesus wherever they are, in whatever they are doing.

I am very excited about Jen's book *Your Defining Moment*. Her revelation of the Church's purpose reaches across cultures, generations, and genders and ignites a fire in believers to be the salt and light in their circumstances. As she teaches, people begin to understand that they aren't working for a paycheck. They are empowered by the Holy Spirit to serve as ministers of the Gospel on the "job," whatever the job is.

This book will change your perspective and encourage you to serve the Lord joyfully in whatever you do.

Pat Harrison
President and Founder,
Faith Christian Fellowship International Church, Inc.

This book is a vital tool in awakening destinies and shifting culture as the Church of Jesus Christ rises up! New young voices like Rev. Jen Tringale are emerging to herald this message of destiny and shifting our culture. *Your Defining Moment* will prepare you to step into your destiny and release the force of the kingdom within you. It is imperative that the current generations hear what voices like hers are saying that they may run with it.

Dutch Sheets
Best Selling Author, President of Dutch Sheets Ministries,
Former Director of Christ For The Nations Institute

This refreshing young author has a VITAL revelation for this generation of believers! Your shining path and God-breathed destiny is waiting to be discovered within the pages of this timely guidebook. *Your Defining Moment* is an illuminating disclosure of God's plan for each believer to influence every aspect of our culture and world. With wisdom beyond her years, Jen takes each reader on a journey of discovery outside the four walls of the church into the amazing excitement of a 'vital faith', changing lives on every strata of human existence. An absolute, "I've got to have it!" for everyone that yearns to maximize their life.

Len and Cathy Mink
Len Mink Ministries,
Hosts of National Television Show, *Len & Cathy*

In our years of knowing Jen, we have watched as her words have encouraged and empowered our church family. In her book, *Your Defining Moment*, Jen puts beautifully into words, things entire congregations need to hear. She explains so powerfully that ministry is not something set aside for preachers and teachers, but that EVERY believer is anointed and appointed to minister in the place God sets them. It is our opinion that this book will change not only churches, but entire communities! We believe that this book will empower believers and start a city-wide awakening. We echo Jen, your world is waiting for you to show up! This book will encourage and propel people to do just that... show up and display God's power to their world.

We know that this book will be a catalyst and a powerful resource for individuals and churches who want to run their race, live a life pleasing to God, and ultimately fulfill His call on their life.

Pastors Aaron and Errin Hankins
Christian Worship Center,
Alexandria, Louisiana

Whether speaking to an individual, a congregation or to a nation, Rev. Jen Tringale rightly discerns the fullness of time of events that tapestry destiny and speaks to it with clarity. She carries an ability to see and know and speaks the revelatory words of a prophet. She has an understanding of the times and her voice prepares the way.

Dr. Mary Frances Varallo
International Author and President of
Mary Frances Varallo Ministries

I have had the privilege of knowing Jen Tringale over the last 20 years. Through her early years at Bible College, I watched the gift and calling she carries develop as she emerged an amazing minister and communicator helping so many to define their calling.

She has always had a God-given ability to recognize the giftings and callings within others. Her ministry carries an anointing that brings clarity and propels people further into their destiny and the plan of God for their life.

This book will be a right on time help to so many and will be a vital tool to the body of Christ.

Leigh Ann Soesbee
Soesbee Ministries International,
Prayer Director, Rhema Bible Church

The prophet Jeremiah and King David both describe destiny and purpose that are God-given before we are born. The quest of life is to allow Holy Spirit to reveal that purpose and anoint our gifts, talents, and abilities to fulfill it. Whether your calling is to fivefold ministry or the marketplace, Jen Tringale's teaching will reveal biblical keys that will enable you to hear the Holy Spirit clearly concerning your calling. This book will enable the author of your purpose to pull from you more and more of your potential.

Dr. Tim Sheets
Senior Pastor, The Oasis Church,
President of Tim Sheets Ministries and
Awakening Now Television

Jen is a phenomenal motivator and influencer who brings passion and clarity each time she ministers. We love having her as a member of Destiny World Outreach Center and have watched her ministry expand and reach around the world. Her relationship with God is evident in all she does as you will discover in her new book, *Your Defining Moment*. She boldly teaches on how to overcome challenges in your life to uncover God's divine purpose for your life! We highly recommend this book; it will motivate and inspire all who read it!

Pastors Chad and Marla Rowe
Destiny World Outreach Center,
Killeen, Texas

This is a book written for every person, no matter his or her walk of life. *Your Defining Moment* is insightful, inspirational and dynamic. Prepare to see your life and your calling through new eyes as you read the powerful message that Jen has been given to teach and preach all over the world. This book will be a game changer for so many as we open our eyes to our destiny, our purpose, His timing, the vision He has placed inside of us and the strategy to fulfill it.

Pastors Caleb and Alicia Moran
Metro Life Church,
LaFayette, Louisiana

I have had the pleasure of watching Jen Tringale grow over the past few years into a powerful and gifted communicator. I highly recommend *Your Defining Moment*, as a necessary resource tool for people of all ages who are wanting to discover God's divine destiny and plan for their lives!

Lynette Lewis
International Author, Speaker and Business Consultant

DEDICATION

I dedicate this book first to my mother, for hearing my destiny on that very important day and for being the courageous woman I have always known. I love you.

To my father, for being the perfect dad for me. How could I ask for more? I love you, dad. To my grandmother, Billie Mae Burkart. You were the first writer I ever admired. You gave me eyes to see the importance of someone's story and its power to help another. I love you more than words could ever say. It is the highest honor to be counted as part of your legacy.

To all of my family and friends, each of you have contributed something essential, special and unique to my life that I am forever grateful for and I love being part of this amazing tribe.

To every person who has committed to this journey of destiny and determined to stay the course though sight unseen. This book is for you. For your courage of heart and your tenacity of hope. You are not alone and it is all going to be worth it!

THANK YOU'S

My deep appreciation to all of the wonderful people who have been a part of this project.

To my literary agent, Margo D. Bush—thank you for believing in this book from the start. You are so excellent at what you do! To Harrison House Publishing and the great team of people there, thank you for all of your great work! To my amazing team that came together to get this project finished on time—Kathy O'Grady, JoeLynn Daugherty, Rebecca Eubanks, Artworks Tulsa Photography, Beth DeLemos, Amanda Barnhart, Bethany Carpio and The Winn Group. Thank you to the JTM Social Media Team—you know who you are. Thank you for lending your voice to help spread the word. Love and appreciate you much! My deep gratitude to the Partners of this ministry who empower us to carry the message of destiny all around the world. Your love and support mean so much to me. To my Prayer Team, I cannot thank you enough for your faithfulness in prayer. You continually make the way for me, keeping me covered and clearing the path ahead. Thank you for all you do! To my church family, Destiny World Outreach Center and my pastors, Chad & Marla Rowe, thank you for all of your love and support. To Len and Cathy Mink, thank you for all of your great counsel along the way on this book project. Thank you for encouraging me to push forward with it. Your love and support have made the difference!

Thank you to every reader who will take something from this book and walk into a greater place of understanding of your God-given destiny. You are what makes this project worth it!

The greatest honor of my life is to be a communicator of the love of God and His destiny and purpose for every life. He chose me before I ever chose Him and I am eternally grateful to my Savior for such a love.

PREFACE

She never knew how she got through the day at work, waiting for the doctor's office to call. Even though she was pretty sure she knew the answer, she was holding out hope that she was wrong.

Finally, the call came. The sweet, upbeat nurse on the other end said what she was not really ready to hear: "Congratulations, Jean! The test came back positive! You are pregnant!" As she started to cry, quietly the nurse said, "Oh dear. I guess you aren't very excited are you?"

"I'll be ok," she replied and hung up the phone.

Stunned and alone, she knew she couldn't stay at the office. She called her sister-in-law and asked her to come get her and take her back to her brother's house. She told no one else where she was going. She had no idea who to call, but she had to talk to someone. She had told her sister-in-law that she was upset and needed to leave work. Finally, she called her best friend and blurted out the news. Her friend could tell her what to do! Hadn't she helped her through some of her craziest teenage stunts? Of course, she had also been the one to talk her into those stunts! Her friend told her, "Don't tell anyone else that you are pregnant. Not a soul! I will pick you up tomorrow and take you to get an abortion. You CANNOT have a baby!"

For the first time in Jean's life, she told her friend, "No! Don't you ever mention that word to me again! I can't believe you would even suggest that to me." Then she hung up. She was shocked that she had actually stood up to her friend. She rarely stood her ground with her friend.

She was still feeling desperate. However, she didn't know to whom she could turn. She was still reeling from the news and trying to figure out what she should do when the phone rang. Her sister-in-law told her that her doctor was on the phone. She hadn't told anyone where she was going. No one at work or the doctor's office knew her brother and sister-in-law's name or number.

Jean felt a lot of respect for this doctor. He had been very kind to her. He wasn't her normal family doctor she had seen since childhood. He didn't know her family at all. She answered the phone and the doctor said, "Jean, I know you are upset, but I had to talk to you. Please don't do anything rash over the weekend. Do you understand me? Talk to your parents. I am sure they will help you through this, but PROMISE me that you won't do anything you can't undo."

She was stunned. "How did you find me?" she asked. "I didn't leave my number with your office or give you my brother's name." The doctor was equally puzzled. "I have no idea. I have a plain white piece of paper on my desk with this phone number and your name on it. I have wanted to talk to you since I saw the results of your blood test. I just thought my nurse left this note for me. Jean, I know you will be all right. Please, just talk to your parents."

This hit home with her. She didn't understand how, but in the midst of so much chaos there were three things she knew to be emphatically true.

1. She knew the doctor was right in what he was saying—she could count on her parents.

2. She knew it wouldn't be easy. Although she didn't recognize it was God, He was getting through to her. She HAD to have this baby.

3. She knew that an angel had to have put that piece of paper on the doctor's desk so he could reach out to her at just that moment.

Even though Jean wasn't serving God at that time, He made Himself heard and He sent that doctor to reassure her that things would be all right. This was a defining moment in my life.

Jean was my mother. She was only nineteen years old and was working for one of the largest advertising agencies in the country producing T.V. commercials in Los Angeles and New York. She was poised to achieve success and enviable status, all before her twenty-first birthday. The odds were stacked against my life even before I took my first breath.

At that moment and time I couldn't fight for my destiny, but God could and He did. He got through to my mother and she fought for me against all of the pressure, the "what if's" and the uncertainty. Sometimes your defining moment comes at great risk, but if you don't trust God, you will never know all that He has planned for your life. He makes all things beautiful.

> All around
> Hope is springing up from this old ground
> Out of chaos life is being found in me
> You make beautiful things
> You make beautiful things out of the dust
> You make beautiful things out of us

"Beautiful Things," recorded by Nicole Binion

"Jen and her mom"

1

DEFINING YOUR CALLING

The World Is Waiting on You to Show Up

For the most part, I grew up in a Spirit-filled, non-denominational church. I had no idea someone could be called to make an impact for the kingdom of God outside a pulpit or without being sent overseas as a missionary. That idea was completely foreign to me. I believed you either served in the church or you worked outside the church in the secular world, and never the two shall meet!

The prevailing thought as I was growing up, in most mainline churches and amongst my close circle of Christian friends, was that the world was evil. You were supposed to stay out of the world or it would get on you. I believe as a result of that thinking, our culture has rapidly declined over the past forty years in every area. Could it be because there was no influence of the kingdom of God present in society? Our light was hidden under a bushel and the bushel in which we were hiding was the church!

As believers, we have grown very skilled at functioning in our church services and inside the walls of the church. However, a lack of understanding about how to influence the world while functioning in it has led us into a type of darkness of our own. Consequently, the world we've been given charge of has paid the price and now, so have we. Much has been taught about those gifts which predominantly function behind pulpits. Those gifts are visible to us on our church platforms. But there has been little taught about the callings and anointings that function outside of the church, yet the church is filled with dedicated, very skilled believers who serve in the marketplace. Their calling is through their vocation which functions outside the walls of the church in the secular world where the hurting, wounded and lost are found.

What exactly are those vocational callings? How do they operate? I have had the privilege of enjoying personal relationships with a few extremely talented musical artists. They were raised in church and worked hard at fine-tuning their talent. When they got their big break, they headed into the mainstream music business and found skyrocketing acclaim. Some performed on award shows and toured on high grossing concert tours. They have entertained thousands, some millions. In the end, they got their clocks cleaned, so to speak, spiritually and emotionally. Those very talented and anointed musicians walked straight into the lion's den without adequate spiritual training or understanding of who they were. They weren't prepared to function in that environment, let alone influence it. They did not go with the crucial support and prayer backing of a local church. Thankfully, those talented friends of mine found restoration. They found pastors who would minister to them just as a person, who were unaffected by their fame or stardom.

It seems some believers have excused themselves from the everyday sense of mission, assuming the task was placed only upon those standing in one of the fivefold offices to make "the kingdoms of this world ... the kingdoms of our Lord" (Revelation 11:15 KJV). My own assumption as a young believer was that as a Christian, my purpose was to live a godly life, give tithes and offerings, attend church every time the doors were open and plod along faithfully. In fact, I remember thinking to myself, *Thank God I know I am called to the ministry because there is no way I could live a life that boring!*

> *"What is the activity of God in your generation and how is He inviting you to join?"*
> Dr. Lance Wallnau

As a ten-year-old girl, I remember reluctantly attending a church camp at my parents' insistence. The location was four hours away from my home in the middle of nowhere in the cornfields of Indiana. The kids in our church joined kids from many other churches in our region, and it was apparent there was no way I was getting out of it. Little did I know at the time, destiny was waiting for me there and would change my life forever.

That week at camp, I had been having a fairly good time staying busy with lots of activities during the day and services at night. However, towards the end of the week, the directors of the camp came to address us. We gathered in a huge barn that had been remodeled and converted into a sanctuary. That night, the speaker taught us about the call of God. He went through the Bible giving examples of how God called Moses, David, Esther and the twelve disciples. He explained how each of these people gave their lives to the call. Something the man said ignited my heart and I could feel the presence of God so intensely that tears ran down my face. I remember my little heart pounding so strongly in my chest that I was embarrassed to think other kids around me might hear it. I had never encountered God speaking to me so strongly. I could feel something like electricity running through my hands.

At the end of the message, the speaker gave an altar call for those who felt God was calling them into the ministry. I shot out of my chair and joined the others up front. I encountered God that night in a way I never had before. It seemed the person God created me to be was ignited on the inside of me. That night I realized God had marked me, although I didn't understand exactly what that meant. As a ten-year-old little girl, I had no idea what ministry was. However, I was very clear about one thing: My life was not my own! God created me with purpose, and I was to use my life to fulfill it. That was one of the first moments in my life where time and destiny met and I was never going to be the same.

Years later after graduating from Bible college, I accepted a position at a church in Ohio as a youth pastor. I always had a good rapport with teenagers but had never aspired to be a youth pastor. That was new territory for me. Although I didn't specifically feel called to be a youth pastor, I knew in my heart it was my assignment at the time and I was given the grace to do it. That was another defining moment in my life that would become very significant.

I desired every teenager to have the same kind of reference point with destiny that I had. Looking back, I realize what a great blessing that was for me, at just ten years old, to have some understanding of what I was called to do. That knowledge set a benchmark that helped me in making every major decision of my life.

When it came time for decisions on relationships, college and a career path, I was able to measure my options with the strong call of God in my heart as I asked myself, "Does this line up with what I am called to do?" That is what I wanted these teenagers to experience. However, as I stood in front of my youth group, it suddenly occurred to me that not all of them were going to be called into the five-fold ministry. At best, there may have been ten percent who had that type of calling. How was I going to motivate and inspire the rest of them? In the paradigm I was in at the time, the lack of a five-fold ministry calling left you solely with the life long obligations of church attendance, giving your tithe and offerings and volunteering in the nursery! Try motivating teenagers with that rendition of Christianity! Tell them that, and they would be back down at the club in a split second. Of course, that is not all there is, and God didn't leave me there. He pushed me into a place of deeper study and what came out of it was a defining moment for all of us. God is the Master Planner! In fact, He has never been caught without a plan!

*"I therefore, the prisoner of the Lord, beseech you
that ye walk worthy of the vocation wherewith ye
are called."*

Ephesians 4:1 KJV

For many years, the prevailing thought has been that this
sense of divine vocation was reserved for the spiritual aristoc-
racy. However, Dr. Timothy Sheets states the word translated
as *calling,* in the Greek, is defined as "a divine invitation to
employment, to vocation."

This is not to take away from, nor diminish the value of
the five-fold ministry gifts. These gifts are to prepare the body
for the work of the ministry. They equip the saints. The more
these ministry gifts are honored and given place to function,
the more increase will come into
your life, your church and your
ministry. The equipping work they
do has a purpose and that purpose
is you. As Pastor Bill Johnson puts
it, "For the believer, there is no
such thing as secular employment. Every believer is in full-
time ministry. Only a few have pulpits in sanctuaries."

**For the believer, there is
no such thing as mere
secular employment,
only vocational calling.**

When we think of men and women of great destiny and
calling, we typically think of those people who have helped to
shape the events of history. In general, mainline Christianity
failed to bring a sense of divine mission down to the man on
the street. It seems that our culture has become such a circus
of propaganda, larger than life personas and image branding,

that we fail to recognize the strong prevailing influence of the everyday person.

While delivering a speech on August 30, 1943 in Quebec, Winston Churchill said, "The strength of a nation is in such simple folk to whom it is given to know each day what is their duty." When the apostle Paul wrote in Ephesians that we should "walk worthy of the vocation" of which we were called, he wasn't addressing church leaders or ministers; he was speaking to the church at Ephesus, a body of believers.

One definition of the word *vocation* is "a call or a summons." It is also defined as "a person's main occupation to which they are suited, or drawn to." Yet another definition adds, "an employment especially regarded as particularly worthy and requiring great dedication."

The truth is, people who live for the purpose of "getting ahead" are different from those who live with a sense of mission and calling. The Christian small business owner, caretaker, daycare worker, mechanic and nurse are the world changers who can create defining moments in somebody's world and change their personal history. Although this may be less dramatic than those who affect the masses and create world events, this kind of work can stretch into a legacy. We are called to be the influencers, the pacesetters, the encouragers and the catalysts for change in every part of our culture.

What is culture? It is the sum of all of a people group's customs, activities and beliefs. Listed below are seven main areas of influence that shape our culture today.

- Family
- Religion/Faith
- Education
- Government/Law
- Media/News & Commentary
- Arts/Entertainment
- Business/Economics

In the United States, Christianity, or religion, has become just a small facet of our culture. Unfortunately, for some it has been deemed an irrelevant part. Yet Christianity is the life of humanity in all its relations to God, and from this relationship, no area of human activity can be excluded. Man's relationship to God is not an aspect of culture. It is meant to be the overlay of every part of our culture to the point that it effects how we work, play and rest. The Church is the body of Christ Jesus and we share in every interest that Jesus was concerned with. That means the whole life.

As I look back on the service that night in the big old barn, my heart is heavy. At the same time when so much was happening within me, I think about the little boy with dark hair sitting next to me that night. He was probably about my age. I remember him as a "brainiac." While I felt electricity in the air, he was kicking his feet in his chair, probably a million miles away in thought. He seemed unaffected by the idea of a call to ministry. My thoughts go to him and I wonder if he was called to be a doctor, a politician or a teacher. That night, nobody was talking about those types of callings. Maybe he was called to be a musician or a scientist, but those vocations that God calls people to were never mentioned. What could have been a defining moment of destiny for many in the room that night, instead went unannounced.

There is much to be done to impact the world we live in. Only a few of us need pulpits in order to do it.

> *"For the earnest expectation of the creation eagerly waits for the revealing (the showing up) of the sons of God."*

> Romans 8:19 NKJV, explanation mine

> *"For the creation waits with eager longing for the revealing of the sons of God."*
>
> Romans 8:19 ESV

2

YOUR TIME, HIS TIME

Life Defining Moments of Time

The moment you are in has provision attached to it. It also has mission attached to it. You carry something that the moment you are in requires. Setting your sights on what is happening now in order to discern what is in your present will prepare you for what is next. In other words, a divinely orchestrated moment never shows up empty-handed! When the right time is recognized and acted on, all of the divine purpose and provision connected to that moment is unleashed.

The life-defining moment of time discussed in this book has its very own unique meaning in the Greek language. It is a specific type of time known as *kairos*. This is my favorite version of time!

Our most common definition of time is another Greek word, *chronos*. We get our English word "chronological" from this Greek word chronos. This speaks of the passing of time and how we mark time. Chronos time or "clock time" is what we measure in minutes, hours, days, and years. The other form of timing, which makes up the defining moments of your life, is kairos. The Greeks call this "pregnant time." This form of time is full of possibility!

Webster's dictionary defines the word kairos as the right or opportune moment, the supreme moment, a window of opportunity or the appointed time. Dutch Sheets, in his book *Intercessory Prayer*, says that a well-timed attack in war would be kairos, or a strategic time. My favorite definition of kairos timing is as follows, "a passing instant when an opening appears which must be driven through with force if success is to be achieved."[1] Simply put, you could say a good working definition of kairos would be when time and destiny meet.

All throughout the Word of God, there are amazing examples of how God sets people up for these kairos moments that become pregnant with purpose. Some of these examples are the ram in the bush at that critical moment when Abraham was prepared to sacrifice his son Isaac. Simeon and Anna were in the temple on the very day, at the very time when Mary and Joseph walked in with Jesus, the Savior of the world, to have Him blessed. They had prayed for years to see God's promise. Queen Esther was placed in position at a kairos moment in order to save a nation in a single day. Even Jesus lived thirty-three years of kairos moments on the earth. These are the moments in life

---

[1] White, E. C., *Kaironomia: On the Will-to-Invent* (Ithaca, NY: Cornell University Press, 1987), 13.

that make movies! They are history-making moments in our personal lives and all attached to our divine destiny.

Someone who doesn't know God might describe a kairos moment as "chance" or "luck." However, the word kairos is used over eighty times in the New Testament. In each instance, it is in relation to a significant event brought about by the Lord himself to move us in harmony with the ticking of His timepiece.

Over the years I have learned three important things about kairos timing:

1. Right timing is not learned, it is discerned. There is more to being able to tell if it's the right time than meets the eye.

2. Paying attention to this kind of timing is essential if we are going to fulfill our destiny.

3. Every kairos moment comes pregnant with purpose.

God does more in these kairos moments than years of labor through chronological time could ever produce!

Coming from a musical family where most everyone either sings or plays multiple instruments, I recognize the significant role that timing plays in music. You can teach a drummer certain patterns, percussive beats and music theory. However, if the person has no natural rhythm, no

Timing is not learned, it is discerned. Timing can't be taught; it is caught.

innate sense of timing, they will forever fall short of what the moment requires.

In the kingdom of God, every time has a purpose attached to it. God's timing, His kairos moments, carry everything that is needed for that moment. That is why it is so vital that we understand the time and season we are in. This understanding can only be discerned by the inward leading of the Holy Spirit. He is the great Orchestrator of the Father's plan.

To wait on timing, is to wait for the delivery of what that time carries. Personal agendas and man-made time frames result in missed opportunities. A person may be dissatisfied with the time or season they are in and may begin looking for what has been purposed for a different time. In doing so, they are missing all that is right with the time that is at hand. God has set it up that if we will trust Him with our times and seasons, we don't have to miss our kairos moments. In other words, in this moment you are in today, you don't need what tomorrow will bring.

First Chronicles 12:32 says, *"The sons of Issachar had under-standing of the times, to know what Israel ought to do"* (NKJV). This was the genius of the sons of Issachar! They understood their times and seasons. Because they could comprehend, they could apprehend what the moment carried.

> *"And thine ears shall hear a word behind thee saying, This is the way, walk ye in it."*
>
> Isaiah 30:21 KJV

I love how this verse from the book of Isaiah describes what it is to "be led by the Spirit of God." He is the One giving the directives that will be your cue to walk into your kairos moments that are full of potential and possibility. Jesus' entire ministry was based on hearing, waiting on and acting out these directives from His Father. Jesus, the Son of God, did nothing without knowing the moment He was in or headed for and what it required. He was not moved by need, by pressure or a desire to guard His reputation. He was not even moved by chronological time!

In my heart I sense a deep, cautionary warning that in our pursuit of excellence in ministry, we do not fabricate and perfect our gatherings to such a place that we have totally removed the element of "kairos moments" from our services. What is so great about knowing exactly how a service is going to go anyway? Gathering to worship a living God and inviting the Holy Spirit to have the preeminence in those gatherings does not lend itself to a static sequence of events. I believe that men and women of destiny hunger and actually crave the thrill of coming to a service where corporately we grab on with both hands to the live wire of the Holy Spirit to discover what He would say in that moment, to collaborate with Him and to follow His directives.

My prayer for us as leaders, is that performance based fears do not cause us to shy away from embracing those moments of having to interpret on the spot what God is wanting to say and do and to collaborate with Him. Some of the most powerful services I have ever been in were those when, corporately, we were all experiencing and following the dynamic moving of the Spirit of God at the same time. Those kairos moments yield a level of ministry that nothing else can produce. What a tragedy it would be if the next generation of leaders was led to believe that the success of any given service was determined by whether everything on "planning center" was executed or not.

A rightly discerned moment can pick you up from one place and catapult you to a new level that would have taken years for you to reach in the natural progression of things. That is the essence, the qualitative value, of a kairos moment or a divine opportunity. Those moments have been prepared for you by your Creator.

> *"For we are His workmanship, created in Christ Jesus for good works, which God prepared beforehand so that we would walk in them."*
>
> Ephesians 2:10, NASB

Those transformative moments present sacred possibilities. Men and women of destiny have always pushed past the limits of chronological timeframes. They believed that the Word of God worked outside of chronological time limitations and could produce the miraculous.

Isn't it interesting that Jesus' first miracle was a miracle of time? In turning the water into a vintage wine, He sped up what would have naturally occurred through the fermenting process of grapes during the chronological passing of time. But Mary's faith unleashed a kairos moment when she said to the servants, "Whatever He tells you to do, do it." So not only did He turn water into wine, He turned it into a wine that normally would have taken years and years to produce!

A kairos moment is something you sense or discern in your heart. It is understanding the moment you are in and what is present. In life, bad timing costs more than anyone is ever prepared to pay, but right timing can pay you richly.

"But when the fullness of time had come, God sent forth his Son" (Galatians 4:4 ESV). We have heard it said, "the best time is the right time." What a pregnant statement! Just because a dream is present, a vision is clear and the gifts are active, does not always mean that the time is now.

"Jesus said to them, 'My time is not yet here.'"
John 7:6 NASB

All of this points to one obvious reality: If Jesus paid attention to timing, we should do the same. Jesus said to them (to his brothers), "My time (the season for the full manifestation to the nation of what I am) is not yet present." One commentary says of this verse, "The season or opportunity for my final self-revelation pauses, and I pause for an intimation of the Father's will." Paying attention to your timing is something you cannot afford to miss out on. God is ready to show you exactly what you need to know about the time you are in right now.

3

ENTRUSTED WITH VISION

Vision Propels You Toward Your Destiny

Vision is a very big word and yet it is every bit as intimate as it is big. That is because vision is personal. It comes from the inside of you and becomes a part of you. When God opens up His realm of mystery and reveals to you a piece of His heart, it is a defining moment that you never forget! God entrusting His plan to you and I should be treated as sacred.

This interaction between God and humanity is an example of His desire to share His heart with us. It shows how much God has invested Himself in you and me, to the point that He calls us His friends. Because Jesus sacrificed His life for us, God our Father is able to breathe vision into our spirit, speak to our hearts and reveal more of His plan to us. Now we know why sharing His vision with us is so sacred to our Father. It was His Son's death on the cross that made it possible.

It is not hard for someone to come up with a plan, an idea or even a worthy cause, but if an individual has a God-breathed vision, then that tells me they have spent time with Him. Vision comes from spending time with God. Each time vision is revealed to you, it leaves a lasting impression. Whenever you pause to recall it, it is just as real as the first day God disclosed it to you.

People with vision churning on the inside of them carry an ever-conscious stream of thought connected to that vision. It is always just below the surface ready to be jotted on a napkin, sketched out on a notepad or eagerly shared with a friend. A person with a vision rolling around on the inside of them is invigorated by opportunities to communicate it. In fact, they need outlets to do just that in order to keep the vision vibrant. Finding safe places for you to share your vision is necessary. Any time spent sharing your vision is never wasted time, but a wise investment of your time. You are feeding the vision and your belief in the vision every time you share it.

Everybody has something they scribble absentmindedly while sitting in a meeting, talking on a long phone call or simply lost in thought. For years I have done this myself and one way or another, I always wind up sketching out globes—globes of all shapes and sizes. My attempts at drawing in those continental outlines are not always geographically correct, but I give it my best shot! I usually wind up sketching rays of light coming down onto the globe and then back out. I never thought much of it until a friend pointed it out to me one day. I had been unknowingly sketching the vision I had on the inside and didn't realize that's what it was. That vision is to ignite the destiny of God within people of all nations and to see them walk in their God-given callings to influence their world.

> *"Write the vision and make it plain on tablets, that he may run who reads it."*
>
> Habakkuk 2:2 NKJV

> *"Communicate the vision in detail; break it down as best you can so that it will inspire people to action to carry it to completion."*
>
> Habakkuk 2:2, my paraphrase

I found an old journal of mine from a New Year's Eve prayer service I attended many years ago. At the end of the service, God spoke to me and gave me this vision. I was standing on a map of the nations and my feet were aflame. I saw myself step on a nation and that fire went outward from my feet and spread across the nation, then I stepped onto another nation and the fire went outward to that nation. It seemed like every time I took a step, the pace quickened and pretty soon I was running back and forth from nation to nation. That was over twenty years ago. Since then, I have taken teams into the nations on more than thirteen international outreaches and have received invitations from many other nations asking me to come to them. It is obvious the pace is picking up and God is opening some amazing doors of opportunity!

I often encourage people who come to me saying they are asking God for vision to look and listen to what's already been coming out of them. Typically, whatever you have compassion for is what you are called to do something about. Out of the abundance of the heart, the mouth speaks (Matthew 12:34). The mouth is the heart's voice, so listen to what you are saying, writing or sketching. The vision is trying to get your attention!

The Bible tells us in Proverbs 29:18 that without vision, the people perish. I have witnessed this in the lives of others and it is painful to watch. Sometimes it is a slow perishing. For example, depression, heaviness, and isolation are all types of a slow perishing. Many times these can be traced back to a loss of vision.

If this principle of vision is true in the negative, then it is also true in the positive. If without vision people perish, then with vision people flourish! Vision propels you. It takes you past the "what" and motivates you to search out and discover the "how." Vision gives wings to your faith and ignites your inspiration. It makes you want to speak to mountains or step out of a boat and walk on the water. It calls you beyond yourself and into that place you have seen on the inside of you. It fuels your determined belief that it will come to pass.

If without vision people perish, then with vision people flourish!

Vision is a very powerful thing. Everything requires vision to continue to exist and ultimately grow. Individuals, ministries, businesses and even nations need vision. Distributing God-breathed vision is the business of heaven and it is a very important business! God breathes vision into a man or a woman and they become carriers of that vision. When they speak it, it sets off a reciprocal effect. When others hear the vision, it ignites something within them.

Once someone hears the vision, the part they play within that vision begins to come alive inside of them. What they hear stirs up the gifts and callings within them. Like a light bulb coming on inside of them, they know they have a part to play!

Vision is dynamic; it causes people to rise up and do unusual things. It has caused some people to sell all of their belongings and move to another city. Some have given large amounts of money, donated a great deal of their time, and offered up their services and talents without charge because they believe in the vision and they want to see it become a reality.

Vision speaks for itself. Vision asks a lot of us, but the rewards are extremely satisfying. Real vision makes us grateful for the opportunity just to be a part. Building the kingdom of God requires visionaries who will risk big, give big and believe big! God has always worked this way and is constantly looking for those who will partner with His vision.

True visionaries are not cultivated in classrooms, but in the presence of God. Habakkuk 2:3 says, *"For the vision is yet for the appointed time; it hastens towards the goal and it will not fail. Though it tarries wait for it; for it will certainly come, it will not delay"* (NASB).

Wait For It

Waiting is typically not something most of us handle very well! But the truth is, vision comes in the waiting and at just the right time. This isn't merely a standing around waiting and it's not the simple passing of time. This waiting is when you suspend all other responsibilities and roles just to be with God, where He is the only agenda. The reason you are there is to inquire after the King's heart. This is the waiting!

Making room in your life for His presence is the catalyst for receiving vision. It is the by-product of a close encounter with a supernatural God. Whether it's vision for your day, your life or your ministry, vision determines where you are going. I realized that vision is not something I can live without and I also can't afford to let the vision slip from before my eyes. Something this powerful and this directional inside of you needs to come from the right place. I don't want anything but heaven supplying my vision!

Ralph W. Sockman said, "Better than speed of action is an accurate sense of direction!" To receive the vision God has for us, even for the day, we need to make ourselves habitually available to Him. He needs to have direct access. Most of the time it is "busyness" that robs us of time with God and cuts off our vision. That is why it's imperative that we protect the time and the place that we spend with God. Without spending quality time with God, even the vision we once had will begin to diminish. The chances are greater that you may stray off course and end up somewhere you had no intention of being. If that happens, get yourself back in that place with Him and He will make all things new and breathe life back into the vision. Guard your intimacy with Him and by doing so, you will be guarding your vision too.

I know that for most people, this process requires some time. It requires stillness. It requires listening to our heart and what the Spirit of God may be saying or revealing. For me, God often reveals things in pictures. I tend to *see* what He is revealing to me on the inside. For others, God may give vision in a different way. No matter how the Lord speaks and reveals things to you, it all starts with being still and listening. For years, I have counseled with people who simply believe they cannot hear the voice of God and so they feel directionless in life. It is so thrilling to me to walk them through the process of eliminating the background noise to help them draw out the vision that was waiting for them all along.

John 14:17 tell us that Jesus sent the Holy Spirit, "the Spirit of truth, whom the world cannot receive, because it neither sees Him nor knows Him; but you know Him, for He dwells with you and will be in you" (NKJV). I believe that one of the Holy Spirit's favorite jobs is to reveal to our hearts the Father's plan for our lives. He is a communicator and He is very good at it! The Holy Spirit is revealing truth and disbursing vision in order to mobilize us to carry out the Father's heart.

There is overall vision and then there may be vision God gives to you for something specific for the day. For instance, there is vision that may come in an instant, and the timing for that vision is the time you are standing in right then and there!

I remember when such vision came to me through a dream. At the time, I was on pastoral staff at a church in Ohio. One night I had a vivid dream. In the dream, I found myself walking up a grassy hill and when I got to the top, I looked out over a large crowd of people facing the opposite direction of me. It appeared they were facing a large, outdoor stage. Somehow, I knew instinctively there were about five thousand people there. When I saw the large crowd all packed together in front of the stage, I turned to leave thinking, *Whatever is going on here, there is no way I am going to get anywhere close. What in the world am I doing here anyway?* Then I heard the Lord speak to me. He said, "Go to the right and then walk down the edge of the crowd as far as you can and I will put you in position." It was at this point that I woke up.

As I got up that morning and started getting ready for the day, this dream continued to weigh heavily on my mind. I just could not seem to get away from it. I had no idea what it meant, but it seemed as if I was supposed to do something about it. But what?

As I was putting on my makeup, I could see the reflection of my television in my bathroom mirror. The news was reporting about a political rally for a vice presidential candidate that was to take place in a couple of hours not far from my house. As soon as I saw the report, I knew in my heart that God was asking me to go. I wrestled with the idea for the next thirty minutes thinking, *what on earth am I supposed to do now?* This was all new territory for me. Finally I came to the conclusion that I should just go. I decided that if I was wrong in what I felt like God was saying to me, at least I'd be the only one who knew! I decided I would rather step out and follow my heart than miss it entirely, so I jumped in my car and headed for the location.

When I got there, it was packed! Traffic was backed up for miles. Over and over, I had to fight the thought that I was totally wasting my time. Finally after about forty-five minutes of inching along, I got to the parking area. I parked my car and got in line to go through security. There were people everywhere. As the security agent handed me back my keys and sunglasses, he looked at me and said, "Just head up that grassy hill and you'll see it, although I don't know how close you will get. There are about five thousand people here already." This was starting to sound familiar!

When I got up to the top of the hill and saw that crowd, my heart began to sink. Again I thought, *What in the world am I doing here? This is crazy!* Right as I began to turn around to leave, I remembered what God had said to me in my dream that night: "Go to the right, walk down as far as you can and I will put you in position." *Well, I have come this far I thought. I might as well see where this thing goes.*

I turned to the right and walked behind the crowd. When I got to the end, I turned and started walking down along the edge of the crowd. I started at the back and kept walking until I got to the front of the crowd. There was still room to walk so I kept going until I came up alongside the back of the stage. I stopped right in front of a line of yellow caution tape and a secret service agent. I paused and smiled. He did not smile back. After a few awkward moments I asked him respectfully,

"Sir, is it all right for me to stand here?" He nodded, but never smiled.

As I began to look around, trying to fight off the urge to run, I realized that just in front of me there was a small winding path that led directly up to the stage. It was only about twenty feet away. After working up my nerve, I asked the secret service agent another question. "Sir, can you tell me if the speakers are going to come in this way?"

He responded, "No, I cannot." *Of course he can't, Jen. He's secret service*! As I nervously shifted around, the agent suddenly stepped forward and leaned in. He said, "Ma'am, I can't tell you if they are going to come in this way or not. However, I can tell you that if you want to greet them, you are in perfect position." Then he smiled. I was in shock! *Perfect position!* That's exactly what God had said in my dream! This was getting serious! Then it occurred to me, *In position for what?* I suddenly had no idea what I was to be in position for!

Now this is where you have to be in a relationship with God in order to hear His voice clearly and instantly, so that you don't miss your defining moments. On the inside I began to pray, "Lord, You have got to show me now what You are orchestrating here. I have walked it out as far as I have seen, and now I need to know the rest." Inspiration from the Holy Spirit began to come. He reminded me of the verse in 1 Samuel 17 when David was being reviled by his oldest brother Eliab as he asked him, "Why have you come down here? With whom did you leave your lowly tasks? For I know how conceited you are and the pride of your heart. You came down just because you wanted to see the battle." David responded, "What could I have done wrong here, for is there not a cause?"

As the Lord continued to speak to my heart standing there in that moment, it all began to fall into place why I was there. Regardless of political party or policy stance, I knew that candidate was a born-again believer and that the family of the candidate had come under severe personal attack. I had an understanding that in that moment, I was there to strengthen and encourage not so much the candidate, but the person. The Lord said to me, "I want you to let them know that you are praying for them and remind them of My Word and My promise to steady them and their family today." I was there on assignment and now I knew what that assignment was.

It seemed to all happen in a flash. Suddenly, a caravan of black SUV's pulled up. The speaker of the house, local officials and one of the state senators got out. Then the vice presidential candidate got out of the vehicle and they all began to walk down that little pathway straight toward me. As they drew near, the hand shaking began.

When the candidate approached me, I took a deep breath. I said, "Governor, I would just like you to know that I am praying for you and your family." She thanked me. I continued, "Specifically I am praying Psalm 5:12, that you would be surrounded like a shield."

She paused and looked at me, still gripping my hand she said, "That's a really good one."

I replied, "Yes, ma'am, it is." She didn't move as it became obvious something bigger than a momentary meet and greet was taking place. "Also," I continued, "I believe the Lord wants me to remind you of what David said to his accusers when they reviled him and came against him. His response was clear, 'Is there not a cause?' And the Lord also wants you to know today that He is taking care of you and your family."

She just stood there staring at me as her eyes began to fill with tears. In that moment, it felt to me as if we were in a bubble and no one could hear us. Still gripping my hand, she leaned in and whispered, "Thank you so much for that. Please keep praying."

I replied, "Yes, ma'am, of course. I sure will."

At this point her security detail was starting to gather. I am sure they were wondering who was holding up the governor as five thousand cheering people waited for her to take the stage. After a hug and, of course, a quick picture, she thanked me again sincerely and took the stage to a deafening cheer from the crowd.

I turned to leave. I had done my part. Like something out of a movie, with five thousand people cheering the people taking the stage, I walked out the same way I had come in and returned to my car. By the time I got in and shut the door, I was shaking and speechless. It seemed so surreal and yet it all played out like clockwork.

I sat in awe and wondered later about all that God had entrusted me with, giving me that dream to get me to that particular place and time. He showed me just where to stand in order to deliver a scripture and a reminder of His promise to someone on the front lines that all was well and they were going to be ok. Later, I found out that someone had accosted her youngest daughter on the sidewalk while she attempted to walk to school. The candidate had to pull her daughter out of school for a time. During the same time, arsonists victimized her family's home church and they almost lost the whole building. No wonder God was sending encouragement! I am sure I was not the only one that He used that way, but I was honored to be a part.

There are times when the vision God gives us will require some extraordinary things, but He is ever working to do the extraordinary to get us what we need in the moment we need it. Remember, vision isn't ever about you, but about what God wants to do through you if you will give Him access.

Give attention to your vision. Take time to make it plain. Do something about it. Go back to the Giver of all visions and hold it up to Him. Ask Him what He has to say about it. Vision is always speaking if you will listen for it. In fact, whatever vision you have on the inside of you is more than likely speaking some things right now that you need to hear today.

4

INSIDE INFORMATION

Divine Revelation Awakens Our Heart

The most powerful person at the negotiating table is the one who holds inside information. Having inside information gives you a winning advantage. In fact, it has been said that the hottest commodity of the twenty-first century is not money but information. He who holds the information will eventually control the money.

When a person has inside information, they are confident and at ease because they are working from a position of power. Having inside information puts you in a position to advance. In much the same way, divine revelation is like having inside information. It illuminates our understanding and brings an inner glow to our mind and spirit. Divine revelation awakens our heart to the knowledge of God and His nature. Revelation from heaven empowers you and positions you, giving you the upper hand to handle anything that comes your way.

Jesus told Peter in Matthew 16:17, *"Blessed are you, Simon Barjona, because flesh and blood did not reveal this to you, but My Father who is in heaven"* (NASB). Jesus also said in John 16:13, *"I still have many things to tell you, but you can't handle them now. But when the Friend comes, the Spirit of the Truth, he will take you by the hand and guide you into all the truth there is"* (Message Bible).

The word "reveal" means to unveil. It involves removing a cover from something that is concealed.

> *"But when He, the Spirit of truth, comes, He will guide you into all the truth; for He will not speak on His own initiative, but whatever He hears, He will speak; and He will disclose to you what is to come."*
>
> John 16:13 NASB

> *"...and He will make known the future to you."*
>
> John16:13 Weymouth's New Translation

> *"...He will speak, and the coming things He will tell you."*
>
> John 16:13 Young's Literal Translation

There is no sign posted on the door to divine revelation that says, "Ministers Only." There are no special credentials needed to have access to this realm of understanding. Divine revelation is no respecter of persons. It is for every believer to obtain. In fact, there is a lot of similarity between the scientist's flash of discovery, the intuitive insight of the artist and the inspired proclamation of the preacher. These are all counted among those to whom God will reveal Himself, if they are open to Him.

Dr. Emil Brunner, professor of theology at the University of Zurich, while visiting at Princeton University, was quoted as saying, "Revelation is such knowledge of the Divine Will as cannot be found through submersion in myself or in the secret of the world, but comes through an act of communication from outside our own range, in which God gives to us of Himself."

When the Bible states "deep calls unto deep" (Psalm 42:7), it is speaking of the vast realm of divine revelation that is too large to inventory. However, as glimpses are given, it stimulates our hearts to search further. You and I then become the inheritors of this understanding and stewards of the mysteries of God.

A dear friend and mentor of mine who has now moved to heaven, Reverend Karen Mosely, once said, "There are never-ending and ever-increasing realms and rooms in God to increase us from faith to faith and glory to glory."

Jesus is the Supreme Revelation of God. He is the Word of God and all proceeding revelation must line up with His word. Divine revelation is progressive and we use the Scriptures like keys to unlock it. It is the Holy Spirit, the third Person of the Godhead who is the Great Revealer. *For all who are being led by the Spirit of God, these are sons of God* (Romans 8:14 NASB).

How Does Divine Revelation Come?
Position:

Divine revelation only comes to those who understand its value enough to be looking for it and who have made the quality decision to lean not to their own understanding, but in all their ways acknowledge Him (Proverbs 3:5-6).

Why is it that one person can sit in a church service and receive divine revelation from heaven while the person sitting right next to them leaves thinking, "What was so great about that?" The answer is in the attitude they possess when they approach. The goal of any minister is to reveal God, but no one can open the door to another's heart for him. It is the attitude of my heart that bends my will to want the will of God. The will of God must have my vote before I can get its vision. My willingness to bend to God's will can't just be about things in the distant future, but must also include those things that would demand action of me in the moment.

The Word of God tells us in Proverbs 3:5-6 to lean not to our own understanding, but in all our ways acknowledge Him with the result being that He will direct our paths. What an incredible collaboration with the Spirit of God! He is the revealer of all truth. He shows us things to come. He is there to lead and guide us into our divine destiny. When we keep close to God, we stay ahead of the calendar!

Atmosphere:

Divine revelation can come in a flash of inspiration, a knowing on the inside or a picture you see in your heart. It can come seemingly out of nowhere in a flash when you are in the right atmosphere. Suddenly, you know what you did not know before. Some atmospheres are so conducive to receiving divine revelation that it seems to hang in the air like electricity. This is the manifest presence of God. A person is carried beyond the usual range of their thoughts and arrives at insights, which are given from the higher wisdom of the Spirit of God. This is the Holy Spirit illuminating our spirit and communicating to us a supernatural wisdom. Once received, we then are responsible for this supernatural wisdom that we now possess.

Sometimes God will draw you to a specific place where you can hear. God led Jeremiah this way.

> *"The word which came to Jeremiah from the Lord saying, 'Arise and go down to the potter's house, and there I will announce My words to you.' Then I went down to the potter's house, and there he was, making something on the wheel."*
>
> Jeremiah 18:1-3 NASB

There have been times when I felt compelled to be at certain meetings, conferences or church services. It was when I was sitting in that atmosphere that the revelation I needed came. Revelation is not something you chase, it is something God orchestrates. Following those leadings is imperative to reaching your destiny. There have been times when it required a great deal of effort and finances on my part to get to some of those places where God was leading me, but the reward was far greater than the cost.

> **Revelation is not something you chase, it is something God orchestrates.**

I could not see exactly how it would pay off at the time but what I could see was the necessity of divine revelation for my life. I knew I would be blessed because of it and it would empower me to succeed. I can honestly say that getting to the place where I received revelation has never failed to pay off!

Preparation:

Divine revelation coming from a charged atmosphere is just one of the ways this great exchange takes place. To paint a picture of another way divine revelation can come, we need to examine a story out of the pages of history. I have always had a love for history, especially early American history from the founding of our nation through the years leading up to the Civil War.

Out of this time period comes a great story about a senator from Massachusetts named Daniel Webster. He was a senator and also served as secretary of state in the 1830's and 1840's. He was also one of the highest-regarded courtroom lawyers of that era. Daniel Webster is best known for a speech he gave, described as "one of the greatest speeches ever given in the history of the United States Senate."[2] The speech was given on the spur of the moment and came in reply to Senator Hayne's stern rebuke of Daniel Webster's viewpoint. Although he had little to no time to prepare, Webster's passionate delivery went on for hours and drew a crowd that packed the house galleries. His reply built an airtight case for his viewpoint and silenced his opposition. People were stunned and wondered

---

[2] Schouler, James, *History of the United States under the Constitution, 1783-1861* (London: The British Library, 2010).

how it was possible that he was able to articulate his thoughts about such a complex issue so accurately and passionately on the spur of the moment.

Later, in Senator Webster's account of the event to a friend, he shared that he felt the occasion had released something that had been building up on the inside throughout long years of study. Webster's passion for the Constitution had been charging his mind and fueling passion for what he believed was the truth. When the moment arose, it ignited all that was stored within him and caused what he described as, "the flash of a smoking thunderbolt" on the inside of him. He explained, "I simply grabbed onto it and then let it loose!"

The words of Webster's speech went on to make an even greater mark in our nation's history when President Abraham Lincoln chose to paraphrase part of his "off the cuff" speech in the Gettysburg Address. Webster's words were echoed as Lincoln declared, "That this nation, under God, shall have a new birth of freedom—and that 'government of the people, by the people, for the people,' shall not perish from the earth." These words have been used over and over again to hold our nation to its origin and purpose.

The example of Webster shows that divine revelation does not only come because of a charged atmosphere; it can also come because of something that has been charged up in us! What we give ourselves to and fill ourselves with can all be preparation for a defining moment when time and destiny meet. When what was once just information is transformed into revelation in the light of the knowledge of God, this becomes "a divine thunderbolt" in our lives. When this transpires, it makes a way in the darkness and causes us to see what we could not see. It is in these moments in church services and gatherings when preaching rises to the heights of prophetic utterance, that people begin looking **with** the ministers and not **at** them.

Someone with a gift to communicate and a charismatic personality may be able to give inspiration, but the prophetic preacher must come with revelation to lift the hearers to a higher place so that they can see. *"My ears had heard of you but now my eyes have seen you"* (Job 42:5 NIV).

Think of the moment when Abraham and his son, Isaac, were on the mountain. Abraham was prepared to sacrifice his only son in obedience to God when suddenly, he heard the voice from heaven that spoke divine revelation. When Abraham heard this voice, he lifted his eyes and looked. There was a ram with Abraham's divine supply. It was in that moment of divine revelation that Abraham saw God as *Jehovah Jireh*, his Provider (Genesis 22:10-14).

Where My Help Comes From

God is interested in taking the foolish things of the world and making them wise. Why? Because divine wisdom gives us opportunities to go beyond where our natural abilities and knowledge could ever take us. It keeps us from danger, leads us to unexpected success, and shows us the hidden wisdom of life that provides an advantage to the disadvantaged. In short, it brings glory to God and points toward His goodness and mercy. It is Him who makes us great!

As Christians, we are not bound to the same limitations of natural circumstance as someone without the knowledge of God. We no longer have to strain, working every natural solution possible in an attempt to work things out. If the answers we seek come from God, then our answers will come from the spirit realm. In other words, the revelation of the answer that we need will come from the inside and work its way out.

Working with Divine Revelation

Scientific study has revealed that there is a reality beyond the sense realm. It is one thing to know that there is more beyond what our senses can perceive, but it is quite another thing to be in a conscious working relationship with this realm. Once revelation comes, you are then responsible to do something with it.

> *"To you it has been granted to know the mysteries of the kingdom."*
>
> Luke 8:10 NASB

Working with divine revelation requires an open approach. If we are only willing to receive things that fit our accustomed thinking, then we will find ourselves boxed in with preconceived ideas. Limited thinking excludes us from experiencing divine revelation. If we are looking for everything to fit in the boxes we have grown familiar with, then we shut out the limitless revelation available to us. All revelation that comes from God will always line up with His Word. His Word is our standard. But we have not yet begun to scratch the surface of all that is contained in God's Word.

Jesus instructed us not to put new wine into old wineskins. He taught that people should be willing to discard traditional ideas in order to receive what He has to give. He explained to Nicodemus the only way to store His truth was to get a new container. The reality of Jesus does not allow for any stagnant interpretation of His work. His work is a new covenant not written on stone tablets, but upon the hearts of His people. His work is His Word. It can all be found in His Word, but it requires a living, divine relationship with Him in order to receive it. Because there is always more of Jesus to see and know, by nature divine revelation is progressive. I believe it is important that each time we approach Him and His Word, we are open and prepared to see and learn more than we ever have before.

When somebody first becomes a Christian, they know very little about God. Catch up with them about 10 years later and they know a great deal more about Him because more has been revealed. In the same way, the church of Jesus Christ, as a whole, marches on generation after generation and each generation ought to be discovering and knowing more of Him and His kingdom. As further revelation comes, we should not be surprised by it.

It is important for us to realize that if there is more to see, then there is more for us to do with what we see. In every new place of revelation, there is a word and there is a work. Revelation empowers us to further produce, peeling back the cover of who He is and who He is in us.

Paul showed us that we are to be confident in the revelation we receive when he said in 2 Timothy 1:12, *"I know whom I have believed."* He also shows his ongoing hunger and expectancy to learn more when he says in 1 Corinthians 13:9, *"For we know in part…"*. Just like Paul, let the fathers of the faith stand strong on the principles on which we currently stand, but may they also lead us on as stewards of the ever-unfolding mysteries of God.

5

DISILLUSIONMENT

Tangled Expectations

Disillusionment on the path to your destiny is not a disqualifier! Have you ever started out with the highest expectations for something only to discover it's not at all what you thought it was going to be ? It is important that you know you have an enemy who seeks to keep you from your destiny. Yes, God has a plan for your life, but the enemy has one too. You and I have been given power over the enemy, but he will still try to take advantage of every opportunity to throw you off course. The enemy's attempts at this won't quit until you leave this earth. When things don't play out just as you thought they would, then feelings of disappointment and disillusionment can cause you to get stuck and want to quit.

In walking out the plan of God for my own life, I have discovered that there are three major traps a person of destiny is going to face that can cause disillusionment. Looking ahead for these things will keep our feet from getting tangled up.

When we know better, we can then do better. But it takes putting the truth to work for us. Let's take a look at these three common areas.

Misplaced Expectations

Leadership doesn't equal perfection. I came face to face with this truth many years ago, shortly after I stepped out on a limb to follow the word of a leader I respected. That leader didn't hold up their end of the deal and the experience left me a little disillusioned and could have taken me off the path to my destiny.

Prior to this experience, in my naïve state, I had assumed that a good leader is always on their game, always chooses the right thing and always works to the benefit of the people around them. Quite a tall order, I know! Thankfully, God took me down a path to help me to understand that leadership doesn't equal perfection. I realized I needed to change my expectations of the people I look up to. God has brought leaders into my life who stuck with me for the duration. When I wasn't on my game, didn't choose the right thing or work to the benefit of those around me, they showed me what being a real leader looks like. I am reminded of this truth every time I am with them.

Remember that the Bible says "God gave gifts unto men" Ephesians 4:8 and in verse 11 it continues on and says, "And he gave some, apostles; and some, prophets; and some, evangelists; and some, pastors and teachers... for the edifying of the body of Christ" (Ephesians 4:11-12). So a pastor or a teacher for instance is not so much a person as it is a gift. The one you call pastor is the person who houses that gift. The same goes for the rest of the five-fold ministry gifts listed here. God appoints people to carry these very important gifts. So the experience you have with the person who houses one of these gifts will be affected by how much their "humanity" has been under the influence of the Word of God. It will also be affected by how much they have done to develop the gift. I believe it is safe to say that the closer you get to the person, the more "humanity" you are going to see. When you see human nature at work, the enemy will try to use that to disappoint or offend you. But when you draw on the Lord for wisdom, His truth always carries you through.

An opportunity like this came knocking at my door when a leader mishandled a situation I was involved with and my motives were called into question. I had gone above and beyond, giving sacrificially to serve. In a moment of anger born out of insecurity, the leader lashed out at me. Everything within me wanted to leave, but as I sat still with God and let His presence comfort me, He led me to His Word.

The words of David from Psalm 35:12 say, "They rewarded me evil for good, to the spoiling of my soul." I realized I was not the first to experience disillusionment while on the path of destiny, and I was not going to be the last. Even David walked through this. I considered how David made the choice to honor King Saul, not for his soulish actions, but for the position he held and the gift he carried. Later, God led me to Psalm 86:5, "For thou, Lord, art good, and ready to forgive; and plenteous in mercy." If this was my Father's mode of operation, then I knew it was going to have to become mine. I learned three valuable lessons that day.

First: *"In your patience possess ye your souls"* (Luke 21:19). Your soul is your possession; it does not belong to anyone else. Your level of peace is yours to maintain, regardless of what anyone else does or doesn't do, and the source of your peace is the Lord. *"For unto thee, O Lord, do I lift up soul"* (Psalm 86:4). This truth has pulled me back from the edge of disappointment many times!

Second: It's not fair to judge every leader by one leader's mistakes. Just because one banker is a thief doesn't mean they all are and to assume so would be ludicrous. *"But every man's judgment comes from the LORD"* (Proverbs 29:26). My role is to let love reign supreme in me and to forgive.

Third: We all have hang ups, even leaders. This doesn't disqualify anyone from service. We are all continually growing in our salvation. However, once you realize a hang up exists, you should be cautious. If the hang up presents a serious problem and makes the person unhealthy to be around, then it is likely time for you to back away. Take the good you can and don't get disillusioned. Determine to continue on the path of your destiny in great faith! *"But none of these things move me, neither count I my life dear unto myself, so that I might finish my course with joy, and the ministry, which I have received of the Lord Jesus, to testify the gospel of the grace of God"* (Acts 20:24).

Disregard for Preparation

Preparation is the art of practicing for what's ahead before arriving at those *kairos* moments. Preparation time is a gift, not a jail sentence. If I truly believe that God has great things ahead for me, then this reality compels me to prepare for them.

There are always seasons of preparation before you step into new places in the plan of God for your life. The Holy Spirit is ever guiding us through these times. There can be preparation seasons of study, learning, serving, training, interning or seasons of extended times of prayer. All of these are setting us up for the defining moments that are coming. When we lose sight of God's goodness and fail to realize He has prepared a good future for us, we can fall prey to negative thoughts and miss out on our preparation time. When this happens, go back and recall the character of God. He is perpetually seeing the best in us and always acting for our good.

Preparation is faith in motion! It is evidence of your expectation that great things await you and you want to be ready! Changing your perspective about your

> **GOD is perpetually seeing the best in us and always acting for our good.**

season of preparation will make all the difference. It can be a chore you have to drag yourself to do, or it can be something you look forward to. You have to push past feeling insignificant in the preparation time. Even though no one is standing on the sidelines cheering you on when you are on the track doing practice runs, drills and stretches, these things are still critical to your success! Preparation time does not hold the excitement of race day, but it is essential!

Preparation means being where you are supposed to be, doing what you are supposed to do, even when no one else is watching to see if you are doing it. On game day when your moment comes, everyone is going to know whether you applied yourself during the days of preparation. Stay free of disillusionment during preparation season by resisting thoughts that you are being left behind while everyone else is in the game. Don't waste your time taking a ride on that train of thought. I can promise you that it will take you somewhere you don't want to go!

The truth is, everyone is in a preparation season for something coming up in his or her life; none of us have arrived yet. It would be smart to make room for preparation in your life and find others who are in a similar season as you. This biblical principle will carry you a long way on the path toward your destiny: *"Iron sharpens iron, so one man sharpens another"* (Proverbs 27:17 NASB). These individuals will keep you inspired and you will do the same for them as you get ready for the God-ordained tremendous opportunities that are just ahead.

Faith vs. Facts

God is looking for water walkers to follow Him. If walking on water were no big deal, then everyone would be doing it. Your path of destiny is a supernatural path. It will more than likely require decisions of you that aren't typical. These decisions do not lead where the crowd is going, either. The sooner you get comfortable with this scenario, the further along you'll be on the path to your destiny.

"Faith is a living, daring confidence in God's grace, so sure and certain that a man could stake his life on it a thousand times."

~ Martin Luther

It takes faith to follow after God. That means forging ahead on the basis of His Word. God is obligated to fulfill His Word. It also means following the leadership of His Spirit. God looks for those who will not measure His words first, nor weigh what He is saying, but will completely trust Him. Reason is faith's enemy; the main job of the believer is to believe. God and man are meant to work in union together, but this only happens in the realm of faith. Walking in your destiny will always require living by faith, and nothing less. Walking half the time by faith and half the time by what natural circumstances or popular opinion dictates will always lead to disillusionment. You can't do it half man's way (by the law) and half by faith. The Bible states clearly that this will make your faith ineffective.

"For the promise, that he should be the heir of the world, was not to Abraham, or to his seed, through the law, but through the righteousness of faith. For if they which are of the law be heirs, faith is made void, and the promise made of none effect."

Romans 4:13-14

"No man can serve two masters."

Matthew 6:24

The best way to live is to follow God all the way. This has always been His plan. Our faith in Him emboldens us to step out of the boat and go to amazing places. Inside every believer is a yearning to see the greatness of God. Our passion is to see His greatness on display through what He has called us to do.

Isaiah 50:7 says, *"For the Lord GOD will help me; therefore shall I not be confounded: therefore have I set my face like a flint, and I know that I shall not be ashamed."* To set your face like a flint simply means that you are determined. It has been said that you can only be as passionate as you are determined. When you are determined, you refuse to give up.

Flint is a very hard type of sedimentary rock. When struck against steel, a flint edge produces sparks to start a fire. Setting your face like a flint means to stand strong in the face of adversity. To set your face like a flint means to regard this as worthwhile when you consider where you are headed. You are headed for days of greatness and nothing is going to displace you from your shining path. His Word is a light on your path of destiny showing you the very best way forward.

> *"O you redeemed ones, on whose behalf this strong resolve was made, you who have been bought by the precious blood of this steadfast, resolute Redeemer, come and think awhile of Him, that your hearts may burn within you and that your faces may be set like flints."*
>
> ~ CH Spurgeon

6

STRATEGY

THE KEY TO SUCCESS

It's one thing to know what you are called to do. It's another thing to know how you are supposed to do it. Strategy comes from the Greek word *stratēgia*, which means a high level plan to achieve one or more goals under conditions of uncertainty.

Skilled strategists are highly sought out individuals. Big business and marketing companies realize that their success depends largely upon the best strategy. History has proven that countries with fewer troops and less resources can come out victorious over larger, more sophisticated armies simply because they have a better strategy.

In today's business world, a strategic thinker is one who can discover innovative and resourceful strategies, which often reshape the competitive landscape. In essence, one who can develop effective strategy provides the competitive edge that businesses crave and success demands.

God has been using strategic thinking since before the creation. His strategy always succeeds, even when it looks like it has failed. His plans always arise triumphant. The crucifixion looked like it was the lowest point in God's plan of redemption. It seemed as though all was lost. Yet all the while, God's strategy was in motion. Through His death on the cross, Jesus became triumphant over the grave. He snatched the keys of death, hell and the grave from Satan and saints of old were resurrected with Him. You and I were raised with Him and seated in Heavenly places. What a strategy!

> *"A wisdom, which not one of the leaders of the present age possesses, for if they had possessed it, they would never have crucified the Lord of glory."*
>
> 1 Corinthians 2:8 Weymouth

Whenever God gives you a dream or vision, it requires strategy to follow. In other words, in order to see the vision come to pass and the dream fulfilled, God's plan must be followed. Following God's strategy for each step and each assignment in your life is the key to your success. Paul prayed in Ephesians 1:17 that we would have a spirit of wisdom and revelation in the knowledge of God.[3]

Increase comes supernaturally when divine strategy is employed. The prophet Jeremiah shared God's promise of success, *"For I know the plans (strategies) I have for you,' declares*

---

[3] McKeown, Max. "How to Think and Act Strategically," *FT Press Publishing, Financial Times,* January 2012.

the LORD, *'plans (strategies) to prosper you and…to give you hope and a future'"* (Jeremiah 29:11 NIV, explanation mine). Divine strategy is revealed when we stay sensitive to the Spirit of God, the Divine Orchestrator. Strategy is a bi-product of being led by the Spirit.

Divine strategy is working with God to achieve the dream He has placed in your heart. I have walked into challenging situations before, feeling invincible because God's strategy was made clear to me. Sure, opposition may arise, but because I have confidence in the plan, nothing can stop me. I am able to face the opposition without flinching. There is a tendency for believers to do what has been done before, just because it was successful. They fail to receive God's current strategy for their assignment. Waiting for God's essential strategies will make all the difference between success and failure.

For over ten years now, I have been leading teams into different countries to hold international outreaches. We have taken more than ten trips to the West Indies to hold evangelistic crusades, medical clinics, and various school events. On one particular trip we even threw a massive party! Some people thought we were crazy, but when we sought the Lord about His plan for the trip, that was the strategy He gave us. "Tell them Jesus sent you to their nation to throw a party and then ask them to come." It seemed crazy at the time, but it was very clear in our hearts that was what we were supposed to do. So we ran with the vision and slowly but surely, God's plan came together. We rented a stage and sound equipment. We hired a caterer and bought what seemed to be every piece of frozen chicken in the entire country! It took a team of over fifty people to pull off the event. These people came from three nations, multiple states in the U.S. and we worked with five local churches. For one week, our teams went door-to-door wearing backpacks stuffed with loaves of freshly baked bread. The team members passed out the bread and invited people to come to the party. It is amazing how the smell of freshly baked bread is a universal language!

The party was a tremendous success. Entire villages came. Hundreds of lives were affected that day as whole families gave their hearts to Jesus. There were untold numbers of healings and miracles. At the end of the trip, some pastors in attendance came to us and said, "You have changed what ministry will be like for us here forever. Nothing has ever been done like this before. It was more than we could imagine." We were not a large, well-known ministry and we certainly didn't have major funding. However, we had God's strategy and with it, we affected a nation in a single day.

When we were planning our next trip to that nation, it was tempting to just repeat the same event. It had been such a huge success and everyone loved it. We knew how to do it. But thankfully we realized the success was not in our execution of a formula. Success came because we listened and God gave us divine strategy for that particular time and for that particular assignment.

Since then, Jamaica and Mexico have been added to our list of countries we minister in. We even hold conferences with church networks in Pakistan via Skype. There are more nations still to come! No matter what happened last year or on the last crusade, we depend on the strategy to come fresh from the Father. He holds the key to the nations and He wants to give them to us!

While I was attending Bible College, I learned of a missionary couple who served in the Czech Republic and Poland. They established Bible Schools and planted many churches. They attributed much of their success to asking the Lord, "What is the key to this nation and what will unlock this city, this region and these people?" They said that God always answered and revealed the key. They would take what God showed them and use it like a key and unlock areas of ministry. What divine strategy! That revelation went deep into my heart as a young Bible school student. I can remember thinking, *If God wants to do that for a nation, He must want to do that with my life.* I remembered the words of Matthew 16:19, "...I will give you the keys of the kingdom" (NKJV).

You win big by using the same methods you used to win small. In other words, it takes the exact same principles to follow God in the small things as it does to follow Him in the big things. You must learn to walk out God's strategy in your own life before you can move into strategies for cities, regions and nations.

What Is Strategic Living?

Strategic living is Spirit-led living. It is living by faith—bold faith. Stick to the strategy, even when it looks like it's not working. There may be times when it seems more could be accomplished faster by doing it another way. Remember that God's strategy has taken into consideration all that your natural eye cannot see. God knows the best path to take. At the base of divine strategy is the layered wisdom of God. The Bible calls it the "manifold wisdom of God."

God is multi-dimensional. He is never just doing one thing at a time. His strategies always accomplish more than one purpose at one time. He is the ultimate multitasker! Divine strategy can accomplish so much because it comes from the timeless place called eternity. God's strategy has no boundaries. There are no unforeseen circumstances to derail Him. Divine strategies come from the Spirit of God and are deposited into our spirits. It is our spirit man that receives them.

Our natural thinking will try to abort God's plan. The flesh wants to follow after what it can see. The kingdom of this world is driven by information, but the kingdom of heaven is driven by revelation. However, our minds are not useless. God has given us intelligence to help us in life. But it is our spirit man that should be informing our intelligence and calling all the shots, not the other way around. There is often a power struggle between our spirit and our head if our spirit man is not developed. God has sent His manifold wisdom into our hearts to develop our spirit man and help us carry out His plans and purposes.

Paul talks about this amazing dynamic of the multi-layered or manifold wisdom of God in his letter to the church at Ephesus: *"To the intent that now unto the principalities and powers in heavenly places might be known by the church the manifold wisdom of God, according to the eternal purpose which he purposed in Christ Jesus our Lord"* (Ephesians 3:10-11). The manifold wisdom of God is always linked to His eternal purpose. In other words, there is a divine strategy from heaven that is linked to you, a divine strategy attached to every assignment He gives to you. Your steps CAN be ordered of the Lord because He HAS put an order to your steps. Those steps will take you into success far beyond what you could have accomplished on your own.

Why do we settle for living as mere men when the manifold wisdom of God brings supernatural results? Our lives should be showcasing the eternal.

> *"Someone with a kingdom mindset says, 'God has a solution for this problem and I have legal access to His realm of mystery, therefore I will seek Him for the answer.'"*
>
> - Bill Johnson

Innovation and Creativity

We cannot fall in line and agree with the morally deprived answers the world offers for its problems. Though we live in a fallen world, God has solutions. There are divine strategies.

Joseph is a great example of a man of destiny who learned to flow in God's divine strategy to impact his own life, the lives of those around him and his nation. His ability to receive and follow the strategy of heaven promoted him, even when everything else was working against him. He was unafraid to follow divine strategies, even though they had not been tried before. In the days ahead, our spiritual and natural leaders will be required to do the same. Following God's divine strategies will be the only way to go forward. We must be led by the

Spirit of God, even if it means doing what has never been done before.

The Purpose of All Innovation Is to Make an Impact

Innovation and creativity must be our forte. Our creative God has strategies the world has never seen. The world is living far below the quality, efficiency and sustainability that God desires for us. Jesus died so the world could receive all that God has to offer. As Christians, we believe that things can be better. There is so much more than what we have tapped into. We must not be motivated by money or status but by passion to see His kingdom expanded. God will reveal to us, by His Spirit, strategies to produce a better living environment.

We need increasingly innovative and creative ways to share the gospel of Jesus Christ. God's ambition is to multiply your potential in this area by giving you His divine strategy. His strategy will always push you to think and achieve big.

History is filled with accounts of those who were short-sighted, who did not make room for the power of innovation and creativity.

> *"There is no reason why anyone would want a computer."*
>
> - Ken Olsen, DEC Founder, 1977

> *"I think there is a world market for maybe five computers."*
>
> - Thomas Watson, Chairman of IBM, 1943

"This telephone has too many shortcomings to ever be considered as a means for communication."

- Western Union Internal Memo, 1876

Obviously, these individuals could not see the tremendous impact these tools of innovation were about to make on the entire world.

As believers, we are called and equipped to make an impact in our world by bringing divine strategies from heaven that are creative and innovative. We are equipped to be on the cutting edge with inside information from God, if we will steer clear of two pitfalls.

1. Becoming married to methods,

2. Comparing someone else's success strategy with our own and attempting to repeat it.

The world is not complete yet. Energy, buildings, roads, education, business, government—our entire living environment can be better and run in a better way. God's plan, His mission, is to drive the revolution through revelation given by His Spirit. What an advantage for Christians to lead strategically with Holy Spirit strategies! Ministers and leaders who bring divine strategy to the decision making table will see sustained growth for churches, organizations and their followers.

How Do You Get God's Strategy for Your Life?

You access God's strategy by His Spirit. The Holy Spirit resides in you. He is the revealer of all truth. He is the spirit of wisdom.

> *"For he that speaks in an unknown tongue speaks not unto men, but unto God: for no man understandeth him; howbeit in the spirit he speaketh mysteries (strategies)."*
>
> 1 Corinthians 14:2, explanation mine

When you pray in the spirit or in other tongues, you speak the language of the Eternal. You are accessing His realm of mystery. Although your head may not understand the process, the Holy Spirit will give you eyes that see and ears that hear.

His plan, His leading, My destiny.

As you continue in your heavenly prayer language, things will begin to become clear. If you will follow, He will lead you into all the answers for all the decisions you have to make. Seek and you will find, knock and it shall be opened. His strategy is not hidden from you. It is there for you to discover and to reveal to those you are called to lead and influence.

Here is an excerpt from my own journal when the Lord encouraged me to live by His divine strategy, "Take time with Me and soon you will see, I'm leading you right into that which you're destined to achieve. Believe Me and win. Believe Me and those whom I send, and you will prosper in the way that you are sent."

Success is not for status; it is for service! That's why we should never be afraid of it. Success is not a dirty word. It's a kingdom word. You were meant to have good success. You were made in God's image and in His likeness, to dream and to achieve. To believe and to see. To understand and then to command. This is the way of the believer. This is who we are and how we are meant to be. We are to live by God's divine revelation and strategies. That is how we will see His Kingdom come and His will (strategies) be done on earth as it is in heaven.

When people ask me how I've stepped into all the divine places I've been in, my answer is simply, "His plan, His leading, my destiny."

7

DIVINE CONNECTIONS

Developing the Art of Collaboration

People cross our paths every day. In the book, *Psychology and the Human Dilemma*, by Rollo May, a psychologist's study estimates that in our western culture, we have anywhere from five hundred to twenty-five hundred acquaintances in our lives each year! That is a lot of people!

What Is a Divine Connection?

Webster's Dictionary defines "divine" as coming from or proceeding directly from God. It also defines "connection" as a relationship in which a person, thing or idea is linked or associated with something or someone else. It can also be an arrangement to execute orders or advance the interests of another.

Divine connections are so thrilling when they happen. It is more than mere chance. You soon realize that what you thought was an out-of-nowhere experience of two people connecting is in fact something much bigger. These defining moments are times you never forget!

Making divine connections is a key strategy of heaven. It is one way in which God orchestrates His master symphony on earth. Divine connections are found throughout the Word of God. Even Jesus' earthly ministry involved a series of divine connections. Some were for a particular moment, others were for a lifetime, but all were significant.

Family relation connected Jesus and John the Baptist as cousins, but they were also connected in their callings. In fact, John the Baptist played a significant role in the launching of Jesus' earthly ministry when he announced who Jesus was and baptized Him in the Jordan River. This shows that although you can be connected to someone in a natural sense such as family, there can also be an overlay of connection for kingdom purposes beyond that. These connections are rich and rewarding, but often require extra protection from attacks that will attempt to disassemble such a powerful partnership.

Each of the twelve disciples represents a divine connection in Jesus' earthly ministry. The bonds forged in those relationships enabled the disciples to continue what He started and launched them into their ministries. Lazarus, Mary and Martha were divine connections, each having a special relationship to Jesus, both in ministry and personally. This shows that God will set up connections for kingdom advancement and for the nurturing of your soul. He cares about both.

Open my eyes Lord to the divine connections you have for me..... Whether for myself or the advancement of others.

Help me to discern divine connections & use them.

If Jesus needed divine connections throughout His life and ministry, then so do we. Most people want these types of connections, but don't know how to handle or rightly steward them once they come. The connection is either neglected or pulled on too much and the relationship sinks like a boat when too much weight is added.

Though the idea of divine connections may be shrouded by mystery and intrigue for some, it is obvious that God considers such connections vital to our destiny. In reality, God uses divine connections to advance you on your journey.

The Art of Collaboration

There are different types of divine connections in life. Examples of marriage, partnership, friendship and teams coming together to accomplish assignments from heaven are found throughout the Word of God. There is no doubt about it, your calling is connected to others! No man is an island, even in fulfilling his or her destiny. The person who is always looking for people God placed in their lives to help them advance or whom they can help advance, is someone who is ever accelerating in the plan of God. On the other hand, those who tell themselves they have arrived or have matured to a place where they no longer require anyone else's contribution, become stuck in the dead sea of their own opinion. They become lifeless with no chance of progression.

advance your Kingdom

Leaders and Mentors

One of the characteristics of divine connections is that when they happen, they are never one-sided. Everyone comes out better because of them!

I have had opportunity over the years to work with some great men and women who are tremendous leaders in business and in the body of Christ. However, I had to learn to discern what each connection was for. I also had to learn that while I was learning from them, I also had a part to play by sharing with them the gifts and abilities God has given me.

The relationship of Moses and Joshua is a dynamic example of this kind of divine connection. Joshua spent his early years following Moses to the tent of meeting and watching how Moses operated. It was clear to everyone Joshua was being groomed for leadership. As it turned out, the unique gifts and abilities that God had placed in Joshua were exactly those that Moses did not have. He would need them, however, in order to fulfill his destiny in the end.

At the end of those forty years in the wilderness, the children of Israel came to the Promised Land and opposing military forces rose up against them. Up to this point, Moses had spent most of his days as a leader keeping the people warm and fed while in the desert. He did not lead military campaigns. As it turned out, Joshua was skilled as a warrior and had also trained up warriors around him.

As Joshua led the forces into battle, Moses, with the assistance of Aaron and Hur, stood above the battlefield on the mountaintop and prayed. This force of prayer empowered Joshua and his men as they fought in battle. In this defining moment, it was not one or the other, but both generations of leaders who were needed in order for the people of God to advance.

Moses and Joshua walked in mutual respect and honor. Joshua respected Moses as his elder, the one who let him walk alongside him and taught him. Moses respected Joshua as an honorable man, a student who carried gifts and talents he did not have. I believe it is essential to notice that Moses was not threatened by Joshua, but placed him in position to launch him into his own destiny. Joshua assisted Moses in completing his own assignment. Joshua needed Moses, but Moses needed Joshua too.

Moses was needed to prepare Joshua for his divine destiny, but Joshua was needed to help Moses finish strong. Moses had given his life to establish through Joshua a divine legacy of faith.

> **In a divine connection where mutual respect and honor is present, everyone wins.**

This is a picture of not only the power of divine connection between two people, but between two generations. This is what I call the power of generational synergy. Elijah and Elisha, Eli and Samuel, Paul and Timothy, Naomi and Ruth—these are examples of generational synergy. Whenever this dynamic is at work, great things are accomplished that reach beyond a single moment and stretch out into the future. It is through divine connections such as these that destiny fulfilled stretches out into a legacy revealed. As leaders, we should always be asking ourselves the question, "How does what God is working to establish through me stretch out beyond me?" The answer lies in divine connections. Ask yourself, "Who is my Moses and who is my Joshua?" In a divine connection where mutual respect and honor is present, everyone wins and the plan of God is advanced.

Divine connections don't just happen between mentors and leaders, but also between peers. God seems to prefer to send people two by two. Jesus did so with the disciples. Paul and Barnabas worked predominantly together for a while. Peter and John worked as a team on some divine assignments. Barack and Deborah carried out an assignment that required input from both of them in order to achieve victory.

I have had the honor of being entrusted with some divine connections that I treasure more than gold. When I was just fourteen years old, the cry of my heart was that God would send me a best friend who wanted the things of God as much as I did. He answered that prayer and that divine friendship still thrives today. It is precious to me and I treasure that friendship greatly. God has used that divine connection to keep me steady through more changes, decisions, and ups and downs than I could ever have imagined. It was through this friendship that I was introduced to Rhema Bible Training College, where I attended Bible school. I had no idea at the time all that God was providing for me through that divine connection at fourteen, but I am so grateful that He knew!

Some divine connections invite divine collaboration. In the summer of 1996 in Tulsa, Oklahoma, I attended a Sunday night church service. As I walked out heading toward my car,

I struck up a conversation with a woman walking out at the same time. It seemed like we just immediately clicked! We became prayer partners and eventually the two of us became four as we added two other friends who were hungry for the things of God. We met once a week for about a year to pray.

Typically prayer partners grow out of friendships, but this was different. Strong friendships developed later as we prayed together. Over the years, we kept in touch as some of us traveled in ministry, moved overseas as missionaries and took staff positions in local churches. The connection that God formed with us during those years of praying together had connected our hearts with eternity. There was nothing like it!

For twenty years, through all the changes, we kept our friendship and our prayer partnership intact as best we could. We have ministered in other countries together, led teams into other nations, ministered in churches together, trained prayer teams and more. One of the most amazing collaborations came together when we hosted a Women's Leadership Summit. It was a gathering of women leaders from all arenas of influence for a time of supernatural equipping and collaboration. We have since held two more Women's Leadership Summits with leaders in attendance from the nations of Canada, Italy, Africa and at least fourteen states. Women who were business owners, publishers, film producers, missionaries, pastors and ministers came together in one place!

There was no way we could have known when we first met the divine collaboration that would result from our relationships. I am so grateful and honored to have been entrusted with such a gift as knowing and working with these mighty women of God. I have come to realize that every time I experience a divine connection, I always walk away the greater for it. Collaborating for kingdom purposes is one of the greatest adventures there is this side of heaven!

The Power of Divine Connections Revealed

I have a unique anointing from God upon my life. So do you! We all do. Whenever you and I partner together on a divine assignment, the combining of those anointings creates a force that is unstoppable. There are some assignments that will require the combination—the synergy—of two or three or more to get the job done.

It is so important to know how to protect and rightly handle a divine connection, whether it's with your Moses, your Joshua or a peer.

1. Honor and respect the gift of God the person carries. Remember, the gift is not the person and the person is not the gift. The person is the carrier of the gift. For instance, let's take the five-fold ministry gift of the apostle. An apostle is not a person. An apostle is a gift. Always honor the gift by showing respect to the one who embodies the gift. You may see the flaws of the person, but that doesn't negate the honor and respect you are to show because of the gift they hold. My showing honor and respect isn't contingent upon your perfection. If it is, then our divine connection is doomed to fail. However, love and honor will call each of us forward to be our best.

2. Realize divine connections are a threat to the enemy so they will very often come under attack. Recognize that attacks can come through another person or as an assault in your mind. Head these attacks off by choosing love and believing the best over and over again. Keep a "no tolerance zone" in your heart for thoughts or feelings of insecurity, fear or envy (1 Corinthians 1:10). This is an ongoing process, but it will protect the connection and enable it to continue to effect your life and the lives of others.

3. Let God bring the connection about. Anything that is forced or manipulated will shut down the purpose of God. Rest in the connection and let favor and patience have its perfect (full and mature) work. Understand that some divine connections are for a season or time and others will walk with you to the very end. Allow both to be what they are.

4. Divine connections deserve preferential treatment. Give your time, talent and treasure to these connections and give them the gift of your loyalty in both word and deed. If the connection is healthy, both parties should be advancing. Protect the reputation of those you are connected to, even when they are not in the room.

5. Boundaries in any relationship create a healthy flow of connection. Establish boundaries and stay within them. As a minister, Paul talked about being able to relate to all walks of life, saying he had become "all things to all people." However, divine connections are not meant to be "all things" to you or you to them.

Remembering this will keep things in order. This is essential so you give no place to the enemy to get a foothold.

8

ROAD MAPPERS

Journey of Opportunity

Life as a believer is a quest as much as it is a conquest. It's just as much about the journey as it is about the destination. There have been seasons in my life when I would have paid dearly for someone to hand me a roadmap to help me navigate through what I was experiencing. I had principles. I just needed to know how to apply those principles in the ever-shifting cultural landscape I encountered along the way.

None of us are the first to walk through a difficult or challenging circumstance. The words found in the book of Ecclesiastes are just as true today as they were then: There is nothing new under the sun (Ecclesiastes 1:9). Yet as time moves on and our world expands, there are definitely changes in our turbulent culture, changes which present each new generation with a whole new set of obstacles.

When I was a youth pastor, I was shocked at what my students were faced with on a daily basis. They faced things that would have been foreign to me when I was a teenager. A friend of mine shared a conversation she had with her mother in regards to the dramatic cultural shift. Her mother told her, "I feel as though I have enriched you for a world that no longer trades in our currency."

I could relate! As a young woman completing Bible College, I was venturing out into the world looking for opportunities in full-time ministry. Most of my peers were getting married, starting families or beginning their professional careers, so mine was not a well-worn path. That part of my life felt more like an "urban safari" than it did my "roaring twenties"! I knew I was following my heart and had an idea about the general direction I was headed. However, since nothing I could see really affirmed that decision, I was eagerly looking for someone or something that would. As long as you are headed in the right direction you will eventually arrive at your destination without a roadmap. Having one, however, brings a lot of security, keeps you from second-guessing and guarantees that you stay on course!

It is embarrassing how lost I am, even in my city, without the Maps application on my phone. It's embarrassing because I have lived here for a little over three years now! Although I may not be home that much, I have still had plenty of time to figure out on my own which roads lead to where. Recently, after being away from home for a while, I headed out to an appointment and discovered that the main route I was used to taking was all torn up and under construction. New roads had been opened up to replace it. Feeling a little concerned, I opened the Map application and typed in the address to get directions. The only route that it offered, however, was the old route that was now closed. The app had not been updated and there was no alternate route offered.

After pulling over at a gas station and sitting in my car for ten minutes anxiously trying to figure out what in the world I was going to do, I eventually came to an amazing thought, *I could ask a human*! I was embarrassed that it had taken me that long to realize that even though technology had failed me, all I had to do was ask a real person for directions. The point of my story is, although you may have run out of directions, someone has been where you are headed! Although the roads may have changed, there are those who can point you in the right direction. These individuals can share what they have learned, they have words to describe the perplexities and, most importantly, they know the way forward. These are the road mappers of life!

point me in the direction of my Roadmappers Lord, & open my eyes to those who are counting on me to be their road mapper.

Road mappers point the way from one defining moment to the next. The truth is that each one of us, in one way or another, carry a roadmap that someone else needs. That makes you invaluable to that person. It may be the person who lost their spouse and can't remember what life looks like without them, or the new graduate caught in the gap between the dimming lights of the graduation party and the pressured expectations of beginning a promising career. Handing someone a piece of the roadmap when they have no idea where to go can be like handing a bottle of water to someone dying of thirst in the desert.

May I always lead them on the path You have designed for them.

I recently witnessed the sweetest example of this while getting a manicure at a local nail salon. It was late in the evening. The only other customers were two ladies getting pedicures. They sat a few seats apart, so it was obvious they were not together. One lady was a beautiful African American lady in her mid-sixties. She was dressed casually and sat quietly watching the news on the television screen on the wall. The other was a pretty young woman in her late twenties. She was dressed in sweat pants and a stained t-shirt. Her hair was pulled back in a falling ponytail. She continuously dozed off and on, jolting awake to quickly check her cell phone that she gripped in her hand. I smiled to myself watching her repeat this cycle, thinking what she really needed was a good nap!

The older lady, seeing the young lady awake again, leaned over the arm of her chair and asked the young woman in a sweet Texas drawl, "Honey, how many you got and how old are they?"

The young woman looked at the other lady, surprised at first, then slowly began to smile as she looked down at her stained t-shirt and replied, "It's that obvious, huh? I've got two toddlers and a three-month-old who won't sleep." The older woman laughed knowingly and for the next several minutes, shared secrets from her own motherhood days and patiently encouraged the exhausted, young mom not to worry, that she would be able to make it all work out.

When she got up to leave, the older lady walked over to the young mother, reached down and patted her on the hand. She said, "Don't you worry about it, honey. This part doesn't last long. Soon they'll be grown up and gone and you'll spend most of your time thinking about the sweet days you're in right now." The young woman laughed with tears streaming down her face and thanked her.

What a moment to witness! I was so moved by this sweet exchange that I leaned forward and quietly asked if I could pay the older woman's bill. When the manicurist asked me why I would do such a thing, I said, "She was so kind to encourage that young mother and it touched my heart. So I want to bless her, but I don't want her to know it's from me." After a few minutes of communicating with his staff, he agreed and quickly took care of it.

When the older lady got up to the counter and was told that someone had paid her bill, she stood motionless, shocked at the news, and she began to cry, saying, "Well, thank you, thank you" over and over. I sat still, careful not to make eye contact, not wanting her to know the gift was from me. When she got to the door to leave, she turned back around and said, "Whoever did this, you just don't know what this means to me. Today is my birthday and it's the first one I am spending alone. My husband just passed away three months ago and this is my first birthday without him. I thank you." With that, she walked out.

Now, we were all crying! I love getting to be part of moments like that. Those moments make life so precious and remind us of what's really important.

Your life experiences, the defining moments that have brought you this far, have given you a roadmap that somebody else desperately needs. The power of just these three words, "I've been there," can move mountains in a person's soul and lift them up to a place where they can believe again to keep going.

My heart's desire is to offer the roadmap that I carry to anyone God brings across my path. I never want to undervalue that opportunity or what God can do with it. I try to always keep fresh in my heart what it meant to me when someone did the same thing. When I could not describe what I was in the middle of and someone came along with the ability to wrap words around it and began to give me directions for moving ahead, that meant everything to me. One of the greatest honors is to be a "road mapper" and to be there when someone else is trying to find their way. Jesus relished His role as The Way, The Truth and The Life. He proclaimed to the world that the only way to the Father was through Him. He was declaring Himself the ultimate guidepost in a world of chaos so that we could all find the Father and find our way home. In doing the same for others, we are being just like our big brother, Jesus.

> **My heart's desire is to offer the roadmap that I carry to anyone God brings across my path.**

The ultimate roadmap for life is found in the Word of God. When everything and everybody was going crazy around him, David was grateful for the words that showed him the way forward. His gratefulness and commitment to follow those words still speaks clearly to us today.

> *"I never make detours from the route you laid out;*
> *you gave me such good directions.*

Your words are so choice, so tasty;
I prefer them to the best home cooking.
With your instruction, I understand life;
that's why I hate false propaganda.
By your words I can see where I'm going;
they throw a beam of light on my dark path.
I've committed myself and I'll never turn back
from living by your righteous order.
Everything's falling apart on me, GOD;
put me together again with your Word.
Festoon me with your finest sayings, GOD;
teach me your holy rules.
My life is as close as my own hands,
but I don't forget what you have revealed.
The wicked do their best to throw me off track,
but I don't swerve an inch from your course.
I inherited your book on living; it's mine forever—
what a gift! And how happy it makes me!
I concentrate on doing exactly what you say—
I always have and always will."

Psalm 119: 102–112 Message

Remember that what you have to offer cannot be taught in a classroom or obtained by following a formula. The power is in what you have been a witness of and sharing it will always be instrumental in the lives of others. Jesus commissioned us to be witnesses to what we have seen and heard. To share the gospel, the good news, is to offer your account of His goodness and saving power in your own life. By doing so, the Holy Spirit will find entrance into the hearts of those seeking their way forward. This is the business of heaven. To give out of what you have learned to make the way for another is one of life's greatest gifts.

Summer
to the women
of the well
is a road mapper

9

ROAD MAKERS

Pioneering New Paths

You and I are surrounded by modern day road makers. In fact, you may be one and not even realize it! There is a difference between those who set out to explore something simply for the thrill of the discovery and those who do so to clear a path for those who are sure to follow. Someone seeking a quick way forward will go around obstacles they encounter, but a true leader is concerned with making a straight path so they will remove obstacles so that it's easier for others to follow.

What Is a Road Maker?

A road maker is a type of pioneer. They can be characterized many ways. Let's take a look at a few of their characteristics.

1. A road maker is the first to apply a new method, area of knowledge or activity.

My father was a spiritual road maker in his family. Growing up as a second generation Italian in upstate New York and the youngest of three sons, he came from a predominantly Catholic family. He attended Catholic schools and served as an altar boy in the local parish. At twenty-five, while owning and operating his own restaurant, a business associate introduced him to what it meant to have a personal relationship with Jesus Christ. He became a born-again Christian, received the baptism of the Holy Spirit and began attending an Assembly of God church.

My father's decision to leave the Catholic Church was a devastating blow to his family. The ties of a traditional Italian-Catholic family are strong. It was hard for my grandmother to understand why my father would make such a choice. My father's decision to break free from the fear of losing the good opinion of his family and follow his hunger for the things of God took courage. Walking outside the traditions of his family cost him something for a season.

However, over time as others watched his life and the strength of his marriage and family, they saw the fruit of his decision. My mother and father have been able to share their understanding and insight into the Word of God with family members. They walked them through periods of loss, crisis and major decision-making. In this way, my father has been a pioneer of faith in his generation to his family.

After graduating from Bible College, I tried to explain to my little Italian grandmother my decision to go into full-time ministry and what I would be doing. I tried to find words to paint the picture in a way that she would understand. Her response came from the only concept she knew. "Oh! So you're going to be like a nun!" That was not exactly the picture I was trying to paint! Years later, she came to a non-denominational church I was speaking at in Syracuse, New York. I will never forget seeing my precious grandmother come forward with tears in her eyes to receive prayer at the end of the service. It was both a precious and humbling experience. The trail my father blazed made the way for me to run freely on mine. I have always felt celebrated in my family for the path I chose, as have my other siblings and cousins for the unique paths they have chosen. We cheer each other on as we each blaze our own trail.

2. A road maker is a member of an infantry group who prepares roads or terrain for the main body of troops.

If you are a road maker, the characteristics of those who perform the road making function in the military may seem familiar to you.

- They are trained at a higher intensity than the rest of the troops.

- They are capable of quick deployment and stay ready for executive orders. They are used for deployment outside of their borders.

- They receive priority in equipment and training to prepare them for their mission.

Typically, those who carve a new path aren't celebrated until their job is complete. In the beginning, it just looks like they are spending a lot of time and energy doing things the hard way when taking other "well worn" paths would be much easier. "Why can't you just do it like everyone else? We've never done it that way before. Everyone knows that will never work." These phrases are repeated many times to the ones blazing new trails. This is why road making is not for the weak at heart.

Road making isn't easy work. It's tedious and requires extended hours of concentrated energy. But road makers don't do what they do for the roar of the crowd. They do it because something bigger than them compels them forward, so they press on. Road makers break out so that they can break open. There is a tenacious drive in the road maker like that of John the Baptist. He did not fit in any mold. His assignment did not fit the modern day expectations of religious society, and yet he was called to function in the midst of it. His message, "Prepare ye the way of the Lord" made little sense to the people of his day. But when he got to the end of the path he had been clearing, there stood Jesus. John had been clearing the path that the Son of God would walk as He began His earthly ministry. Maybe what you are called to do is not so much about you but more about what comes after you. This is the call of the road maker and when they heed the call, the results can change things for generations to come.

Road makers break out so that they can break open.

Road makers can be those who change the course of their family line by choosing not to divorce or have children out of wedlock. They are the first to own a home, a business, get out of debt, faithfully attend a church or even start a church. They are the first to break the cycle of alcoholism, drug abuse, depression, cycles of anger, physical abuse and food addictions. They are the first to trust authority instead of running from it. They live to give instead of live to get. All of these are road makers to their generation. They shift the destinies of their family tree by the choices they make, enabling those who come after them to operate at a higher place and move to new horizons of conquest.

3. A road maker is a trailblazer, developer, innovator, groundbreaker or one who spearheads.

Even in the twenty-first century, there is new ground that is yet to be broken up. Breaking ground in a family, ethnic culture, community or profession are assignments from God. He has been preparing those who are His "sent ones" to do just that. If you look around and can't see your counterparts around you, those who are tasked with doing what you're doing in the same place you are doing it, then chances are you're a road maker. If you have to travel long distances to find people who think like you, have vision like you and are compelled to go against the grain to make the way for God to do something new, chances are you're a road maker. If you are consistently finding new ways to take things to a higher level and take others with you in order to make a greater impact, chances are you're a road maker.

The world today is in dire need of road makers. Lost in their own cloud of circumstances or feeling hopeless from the tragedies of the modern world, many today live with no moral compass. They are lost in the confusion of compromises they have made along the way.

Nothing could better convey the need we have for road makers than an editorial that was printed in *Fortune* Magazine. In this piece the editor admits that America owes its ideals to the church, but asserted that the church is no longer leading in holding to those ideals. He criticized church leaders for following rather than leading their congregations stating, "It is the practice of many 'mainstream' churches to bend their messages to the will of the majority." He claimed, "the mainstream church is not inspired and the result is a viscious spiral of spiritual disillusionment." When I read those words, I immediately felt defensive, seeing the editor's comments as a generalized and somewhat blind portrayal of the mainstream church. I felt the church was being misrepresented, but as I read on, what was written next gripped my heart. I could hear within the editor's words the cry for help. He continued to write, "There is only one way out of the spiral. The way out is a sound of a voice, not our own voice, but a voice coming from something not ourselves, in the existence of which we cannot disbelieve. It is the earthly task of church leaders to hear this voice, to cause us to hear it and to tell us what it is saying."

This was printed in the January edition of *Fortune* Magazine in 1940. How much more do these words ring true today? The world has become exhausted with disillusionment, hype and propaganda. They are searching for a voice that rings true. A voice that is genuine in both its answers and its compassion.

A voice that points the way forward. This is the heart of the Father and the purpose for which He sent us.

God gives a clarion call to road makers through the prophet Isaiah: *"Prepare ye the way of the people, Raise up, raise up the highway, clear it from stones, Lift up an ensign over the peoples"* (Isaiah 62:10 Young's). This is our task. To be a road maker is not just the desire of every leader; it is exactly what makes someone a leader.

I believe it is important to note that some road makers are seers, those with prophetic insight. They are the ones who see ahead of the crowd and with their words, they chart the course for advancement. Others are poised to remove large obstacles and lay an axe to the roots of unbelief, traditions of men and antiquated methods. There are those who do the work of pouring the blacktop, laying the foundations and leading the masses to a higher road of travel. No matter which of these you are, if we each do our part and patiently work together, we will see the masses living in a higher place. Tomorrow we will find the crowd traveling where the seer walks today.

10

LEGACY

Our Important Contribution

People who leave legacies are those who have made it a habit to give rather than withhold throughout their lifetime. Legacy leavers are not selfish or insecure. They look beyond their own experience to the betterment of those within their care. They think about how all of the defining moments in their lives will have an impact. Legacy leavers make choices based on a sense of responsibility and consider what they do an important contribution.

This concept of legacy as the backdrop for life's decisions has been the major force that has kept whole civilizations from extinction!

"To live and work for the benefit of the seventh generation into the future."

This phrase originated with the Iroquois Indians. The Iroquois hold it appropriate to think seven generations ahead. That is one hundred and forty years into the future. A guiding principle of their leaders is to determine whether the decisions they make today will benefit their children seven generations into the future. Wow! If only more of us thought this way! However, this goes counter to the popular thinking of a "me-centric" "play now, pay later" society.

The Iroquois commitment to this principle runs deep in the core of who they are as a people. "In every deliberation, we must consider the impact on the seventh generation... even if it requires having skin as thick as the bark of a pine."[4] This was a common saying of the leaders of this Indian nation.

It is pretty interesting to read the original language used to describe their perspective:

> "In all of your deliberations in the Confederate Council, in your efforts at law making, in all your official acts, self-interest shall be cast into oblivion... return to the way of the Great Law which is just and right. Look and listen for the welfare of the whole people and have always in view not only the present but also the coming generations, even those whose

---

[4] *The Constitution of the Iroquois Nations: The Great Binding Law.* Copyright © 1993-2014.

faces are yet beneath the surface of the ground—the unborn of the future Nation."

When I first read this, my heart was moved by the protective sense these governing leaders felt for generations yet to be born. Oh, how this way of thinking would have protected the unborn in our own nation, as well other nations, and served us greatly!

Oren Lyons, Chief of the Onondaga Nation writes, "We are looking ahead, as is one of the first mandates given us as chiefs, to make sure and to make every decision that we make relate to the welfare and well-being of the seventh generation to come. What about the seventh generation? Where are you taking them? What will they have?"[5]

These are questions that require us to look long past the comfort of the day and into another generation's future to determine if our decisions are affecting them for the positive or the negative. As the church of Jesus Christ, both as an organization and as individuals, we should willingly hold ourselves to such inspection.

There is a story of two kings in the Bible that is a perfect dichotomy of a selfish existence versus one who is legacy minded.

The first king had done an excellent job at expanding his kingdom, conquering new territory and providing peace and security during his reign. However, the day came when out

---

[5] Vecsey, Christopher and Robert W. Venables, editors. *American Indian Environments: Ecological Issues in Native American History* (Syracuse, NY: Syracuse University Press, 1994), 173, 174.

of pride and arrogance, he made a series of grave mistakes. Blinded by his own arrogance, he began trusting the wrong people. Upon realizing he had made the kingdom vulnerable by his mistakes, he called together his wise counselors and a prominent man of God to advise him on how bad the consequences of his mistakes would be. Although the others tried to console the king, it was the man of God who delivered the brutal truth.

> *"'The time will certainly come when everything in your palace and all that your fathers have stored up until this day will be carried off to Babylon; nothing will be left,' says the LORD. 'Some of your descendants who come from you will be taken away, and they will become eunuchs in the palace of the king of Babylon.'"*
>
> 2 Kings 20:17, 18 HCSB

The king's response revealed the attitude of his heart, which cared only for his own self-preservation.

> *'The word of the LORD that you have spoken is good,' for he thought: Why not, if there will be peace and security during my lifetime?"*
>
> 2 Kings 20:18 HCSB

He had no compassion and felt no responsibility for what would come after him. The king's conscience was satisfied in knowing that trouble would not come in his lifetime. His was a selfish vision that considered only his own comfort. The descendants of King Hezekiah would bear the brunt for his mistakes as they were taken into slavery by a foreign power, rather than inherit the throne of their father.

The story of the second king plays out quite differently. Although this king was far from perfect and committed some serious atrocities during his reign, the attitude of his heart always brought him back to God for mercy and restoration. As king, he was consumed with the generational promise given by God concerning the legacy of his kingdom. This king was so consumed with it that even upon his deathbed, he used his final breath to remind God of His promise. The last words spoken by King David were, *"That the LORD may carry out His promise which He spoke concerning me, saying, 'If your sons are careful of their way, to walk before Me in truth with all their heart and with all their soul, you shall not lack a man on the throne of Israel'"* (1 Kings 2:4 NASB).

Generations are meant to build one upon the other.

While one king's vision only went as far as his own comfort, the other's was focused on the vitality of his legacy. Possibly one of the most important questions we can ask ourselves is, "How does what God has been working to establish through me, reach beyond me?" This kind of thinking requires a long-term vision and a feeling of responsibility that reaches beyond our own success and well-being. Legacy matters to God.

The founder of my alma mater, Rhema Bible Training College, was Rev. Kenneth E. Hagin. He is a man whom I hold in the highest respect and who many consider to be the modern day father of the Word of Faith movement. He often shared how God had told Him that unless the move of the Spirit was taught to this next generation, the next great move of God would be lost. He spent the latter years of his ministry teaching and demonstrating the move of the Holy Spirit. This was an assignment of legacy given to him by God and thousands are carrying that assignment on today. Giving of yourself for the advancement of others will ultimately be the legacy you leave.

Generations are meant to build one upon the other. *"One generation shall praise Your works to another, and shall declare Your mighty acts" (Psalm 145:4 NKJV).*

There is a current trend among many churches and organizations to take on a persona of being either young or old. Instead of placing value on and utilizing strengths of both the young and old in our organizations, a kind of unspoken generational segregation becomes the status quo. This trend of generational segregation is stifling to an organization's ability to grow and succeed. Furthermore, it is counter-productive to establishing a legacy, almost guaranteeing a stunted one or two-generation term of ministry at best.

Ask yourself these two questions:

1. How does what God has been working to establish through me carry on beyond me?

2. Am I open to going beyond myself in order to have lasting effect?

Have you have ever watched multiple generations interacting? They may energetically acknowledge one another, but many times both young and old walk away a bit frustrated thinking, "They just don't get it!" This way of thinking creates frustration and stagnation in the older generation and displacement and isolation in the younger. In the end, both generations are drastically less effective.

The Cost You Are Paying That You Might Not Know About

When young leaders do not value the influence of older leaders, it can lead to their premature decision to "break off" rather than be "sent out." These isolated young leaders are then prone to leave a wake of casualties behind them because they did not have the safety net that wisdom and guidance provides to steer them to do otherwise. Most young leaders I know who struggle with the urge to "break off" do so out of high levels of frustration as they feel they are being told to "wait your turn" instead of being developed and given room to function and grow in their leadership abilities.

When older generations fail to make room at the decision-making table for younger leaders, organizations are placed in grave danger of extinction. There is no one present to serve up fresh momentum and vitality through creative new methods and innovation (which happen to be dominant traits of the next generation). This hesitation to change typically comes out of frustration felt toward young leaders as older leaders see them as having no real sense of commitment and having a tendency to jump ship too early.

Invest in the Future

Both ways of thinking, which are rooted in distrust and fear, rob us of a great strength. We must cast aside such thinking if we are to have any lasting impact. If it is true that those from the same generation, whether young or old, have the exact same generational perspective, then it must be that we are all required to go beyond our peer group. We need to trust and see through another generation's eyes if we are ever to see days of remarkable expansion rather than show up on the endangered species list! Generational synergy moves those of all ages into action as we interact with each other. This synergy brings the group as a whole from complacency to productivity.

Genesis 1:28 says, "*And God blessed them, and God said unto them, Be fruitful, and multiply and replenish the earth.*" When I stop and consider the original mandate that God gave to Adam and Eve in the garden, I find it contains the vocabulary of legacy. Within the command to Adam and Eve that God gave regarding their life's work, He reveals that part of the work is to ensure that what they establish is sustained.

Strong's New Testament tells us that the word "replenish" speaks of filling up, furnishing, setting in place, giving to (and causing) to overflow. This seems to indicate that the full destiny of what God has been working to build through me must continue beyond me. Part of my calling is to replenish this work by giving what I carry to others so that they can carry it on. By doing this, the work will be sustained and no doubt, taken even further.

It takes the better part of a lifetime to grow and mature the calling and anointing of God to full expression. What these fully matured callings and anointings bring to the world are of tremendous value and significance to the ongoing work of God in the earth. The tragedy would be if the individuals carrying these callings and anointings passed on nothing to the next generation. What if that which they learned went with them to the grave? If the spirit of what they carried was never picked up by others, there would be no continuation of activity.

We have a legacy of faith; a legacy of the working of the Spirit of God that must be given to the generations who will carry it on and pass it on to others as well.

> *"For though you have countless guides in Christ, you do not have many fathers."*
>
> 1 Corinthians 4:15 ESV

Role of Young Leaders

As I follow seasoned men and women of God whom I respect, especially those with whom God has led me to align, I am ever listening to what they are saying and watching what they are doing. It all becomes part of the legacy that is being passed on to me. I don't wait for these leaders to come and knock on my door. I go to them and I glean from all that they have overcome and lived out through faith. I find the more I avail myself to them, the more they are compelled to impart things to me. This is my spiritual inheritance.

> *"We ought to give the more earnest heed to the things which we have heard, lest at any time we should let them slip."*
>
> Hebrews 2:1

I am not looking for a baton to be passed to me. I am watching and listening so that I might come alongside these great men and women of faith. I synchronize my pace with theirs. I watch them and I set myself to run in step with them in faith, in love and in integrity. In doing so, when the day comes that they are no longer here and we are no longer running side by side, I will have my pace rightly set. I will already be trained and will continue to run my race. I will protect, advance and replenish the work of God because I know that another day is soon approaching when I will look to my side and find one running alongside me, looking to keep pace with me.

Everything that God is able to establish through you creates a broader place for the generation that comes after you. You are adding to the spiritual inheritance of the next generation and ensuring that the legacy of faith continues on. It was intended to be ever increasing and advancing... from glory to glory!

> *"Wherefore seeing we also are compassed about with so great a cloud of witnesses, let us lay aside every weight, and the sin which doth so easily beset us, and let us run with patience the race that is set before us, looking unto Jesus the author and finisher of our faith."*
>
> Hebrews 12:1-2

We have received a legacy of vision, tenacity and strength from those who have gone before us. We are surrounded by their witness through the testimony of their lives. Now you and I are being called upon to lay claim to this legacy of strength and power. I believe that we are facing a new moment of opportunity.

What Does This Look Like?

In the book of Joel and again in Acts chapter two, we see the most beautiful prophetic picture that resulted in the birth of the church. What makes it even more beautiful is that after two thousand years, the legacy is still in the making. The prophet Joel is quoted in Acts 2:17 saying, *"And it shall come to pass in the last days, saith God, I will pour out of my Spirit upon all flesh: and your sons and your daughters shall prophesy, your young men shall see visions, and your old men shall dream dreams."*

This was not for one singled-out generation, but for all generations. Young and old, men and women, simultaneously inspired by God to proclaim the Word of the Lord. The result of this initial inspiration shifted the course of history, setting off a wake of thousands coming to the saving power of Jesus Christ.

The bottom line is that we need each other to complete the task at hand. That means that all generations are required to be active. In the midst of an era when distress has reached an all-time high, this is not the time for us to burrow ourselves down into what is familiar and become islands to ourselves. We are the body and we need each other. Let's go together, fathers and mothers in the faith, young leaders and influencers alike, and give to each other that which each supplies in order to see the body of Christ increase and grow. Growing in numbers, yes, but also in influence and in unity, until we make the kingdoms of this world, the kingdoms of our God. This is the defining moment the world is waiting for and this is our time.

ABOUT THE AUTHOR

Jen ministers with a specific anointing to bring clarity and focus to the purpose of God in people's hearts, and she heavily emphasizes how everyone can impact the culture around them through their vocational callings. She shares relevant and time-proven strategies for expanding the Kingdom of God in the real world.

Her easy communication is relatable, conveying these truths in ways that are easy to understand, breaking down the big picture into bite-sized pieces. Embracing a sense of divine purpose on her life at a young age, Jen determined to whole-heartedly pursue the call of God that would ultimately steer the course of the rest of her life. Growing up very active in the local church, her path eventually led her to Rhema Bible Training Center where she graduated in 1997. She also served in the Prayer & Healing Center at Kenneth Hagin Ministries for two years.

Having experience in both the corporate world as well as the local church, she has worked in public relations for a commercial bank chain and served as spokesperson for many for-profit and non-profit organizations. Stepping into full time ministry, Jen served on the pastoral staff in the local church as a youth pastor, associate pastor and media director, producing a weekly television show seen around the country.

In 2004, Jen co-founded a non-profit missions organization, leading multiple teams on overseas trips. In 2008, she was approached to write curriculum on how people can discover their God-given purpose through their vocational calling. This resulted in the 2009 release of "The 7 Mountain Strategy" curriculum, and it has had great success!

She has appeared on such Christian television shows as *Praise the Lord, TBN with Len and Cathy Mink, Make Your Day Count* with Lindsay Roberts and has most recently interviewed on a brand new show to be released on ABC Family next year.

Coming from a family background that instilled the importance of civic duty and involvement, Jen carries a strong sense of patriotism. She has organized local voter registration, met with political candidates and worked with such groups as the Family Research Council, Citizens for Community Values and others.

Jen enjoys being a 30-something woman in ministry. She is originally from Florence, Kentucky and now resides in Fort Worth, Texas.

FOR MORE INFORMATION:

Website: www.jentringale.com

Facebook: www.facebook.com/JenTringale

Twitter: www.twitter.com/JenTringale

Instagram: JenTringale

Booking Info: booking@jentringale.com

Phone: 1 877 286 2995

PRAYER OF SALVATION

God loves you—no matter who you are, no matter what your past. God loves you so much that He gave His one and only begotten Son for you. The Bible tells us that "…whoever believes in Him shall not perish but have eternal life" (John 3:16 NIV). Jesus laid down His life and rose again so that we could spend eternity with Him in heaven and experience His absolute best on earth. If you would like to receive Jesus into your life, say the following prayer out loud and mean it from your heart.

Heavenly Father, I come to You admitting that I am a sinner. Right now, I choose to turn away from sin, and I ask You to cleanse me of all unrighteousness. I believe that Your Son, Jesus, died on the cross to take away my sins. I also believe that He rose again from the dead so that I might be forgiven of my sins and made righteous through faith in Him. I call upon the name of Jesus Christ to be the Savior and Lord of my life. Jesus, I choose to follow You and ask that You fill me with the power of the Holy Spirit. I declare that right now I am a child of God. I am free from sin and full of the righteousness of God. I am saved in Jesus' name. Amen.

If you prayed this prayer to receive Jesus Christ as your Savior for the first time, please contact us on the Web at **www.harrisonhouse.com** to receive a free book.

Or you may write to us at
Harrison House • P.O. Box 35035 • Tulsa, Oklahoma 74153

The Harrison House Vision

Proclaiming the truth and the power

Of the Gospel of Jesus Christ

With excellence;

Challenging Christians to

Live victoriously,

Grow spiritually,

Know God intimately.